SABRE W[...]
MIG ALLEY DO[...]

STEVE STONE

© Steve Stone 2014

Steve Stone has asserted his rights under the Copyright, Design and Patents Act, 1988, to be identified as the author of this work.

Published by Digital Dreams Publishing December 2014

ISBN-13: 978-1517267421

ISBN-10: 1517267420

CONTENTS

FOREWARD 4

CHAPTER ONE 12

CHAPTER TWO 18

CHAPTER THREE 23

CHAPTER FOUR 30

CHAPTER FIVE 41

CHAPTER SIX 50

CHAPTER SEVEN 55

CHAPTER EIGHT 57

CHAPTER NINE 62

CHAPTER TEN 68

CHAPTER ELEVEN 75

CHAPTER TWELVE 79

CHAPTER THIRTEEN 85

CHAPTER FOUTEEN 92

GLOSSARY 97

FOREWARD

The Korean War lasted between 25 June 1950 and 27 July 1953. In all, some 5 million soldiers and civilians would lose their lives during the war. This included the loss of 40,000 Americans and over 100,000 who were wounded. The war began when some 75,000 soldiers from the North Korean People's Army swarmed across the 38th parallel, the boundary between the Soviet-backed Democratic People's Republic of Korea to the north and the pro-Western Republic of Korea to the south. This invasion was the first military action of the Cold War. Although the war was between North and South Korea. A United Nations force led by the United States of America fought for the South, and China fought for the North, also assisted by the Soviet Union. The war arose from the division of Korea at the end of World War II and from the global tensions of the Cold War that developed immediately afterwards. As far as American officials were concerned, it was a war against the forces of international communism itself. In July, 1950, American troops entered the Korean War in support of South Korea.

The war was fought both on the ground and in the air and saw the first jet v jet encounters. It was also the war that saw the final transition from piston engine aircraft to jet aircraft, with a mixture of WWII designs and post war designs being used.

In the early days of the Korean War, the fast, high-climbing little MiG-15, code-named Fagot by NATO, came as quite a shock to the American airmen. Armed with .23 and .37-mm cannons, it shot down a number of B-29s, and forced the USAF to halt daylight bombing raids. The MiG-15 was clearly superior to the American F-80 and F-51 Mustang fighters currently in Korea, although the American pilots' superior skill and training helped close the gap. On November 8, 1950, an F-80 flown by 1st Lt. Russell Brown shot down a MiG-15 in history's first all-jet dogfight.

When the F-86 Sabre, America's first swept-wing fighter, arrived in Korea, the tables were turned. Although the MiG could out climb the Sabre at altitude, it couldn't match its roll rate, turn radius, or visibility. Better-trained Sabre pilots racked up a claimed kill ratio of 14:1 against the MiGs. Dogfights in "MiG Alley" along the Yalu River on the border of North Korea and China are among the most heavily written about in terms of aviation history.

The North American F-86 Sabre was produced by North American Aviation. The Sabre was the United States' first swept wing fighter which could counter the similarly-winged Soviet MiG-15 in high-speed dogfights. It is considered one of the best and most important fighter aircraft of the Korean War. Although it was developed in the late 1940s and was outdated by the end of the '50s, the Sabre proved versatile and adaptable, and continued as a front-line fighter in numerous air forces until the last active operational examples were retired by the Bolivian Air Force in 1994.

Its success led to an extended production run of more than 7,800 aircraft between 1949 and 1956, in the US, Japan and Italy. Variants were built in Canada and Australia. The Canadair Sabre added another 1,815 airframes, and the significantly redesigned CAC Sabre had a production run of 112. The Sabre was by far the most-produced Western jet fighter of the time, with total production of all variants standing at 9,860 aircraft.

North American was already known for producing the piston engine P-51 Mustang in World War II, which went on to become one of the best fighters of World War Two. The Mustang even saw combat against some of the first operational jet fighters in the Korean War.

In late 1944, North American proposed its first jet fighter to the U.S. Navy which became the FJ-1 Fury. It was an unexceptional jet fighter which had a straight wing derived from the P-51. Initial proposals to meet a USAAF requirement for a medium-range, single-seat, high-altitude jet-powered day escort fighter and fighter bomber were drafted in mid-1944. Then in early 1945, North American Aviation submitted four designs. The USAAF selected one design over the others, and granted North American a contract to build three examples of the XP-86 experimental design. Deleting specific requirements from the FJ-1 Fury, coupled with other modifications, allowed the XP-86 to be lighter and considerably faster than the Fury, with an estimated top speed of 582 mph versus the Fury's 547 mph despite the gain in speed, early studies revealed the XP-86 would have the same performance as its rivals, the XP-80 and XP-84. It was also feared that, because these designs were more advanced in their development stages, the XP-86 would be cancelled.

The most important issue that faced the XP-86, was that it would not be able to meet the required top speed of 600 mph. This meant North American had to quickly come up with something that would not only increase speed but move jet fighter design forward. The F-86 Sabre was the first American aircraft to use flight research data seized from the German aerodynamicists at the end of World War II. With North American, being the first manufacturer to make use of this data. The data showed that a thin swept wing could greatly reduce drag and delay compressibility problems which had bedevilled even prop-powered fighters such as the Lockheed P-38 Lightning approaching the speed of sound in dives. German engineers and designers, by 1944, had established the benefits of swept wings based on experimental designs dating back to 1940. Study of the data showed that a swept wing would solve their speed problem, while a slat on the wing's leading edge which extended at low speeds would enhance low-speed stability, as the issue with a swept wing was it increased the stalling speed.

By the time, German data had been looked at, the XP-86 was in an advance stage of design. Changing the wing from straight to swept was met with resistance from senior managers within North American. However, wind tunnel test revealed the advantages of changing the design and it the wing design was adopted. The wing was swept by 35 degrees and an automatic slat design taken from the German Messerschmitt Me 262 jet fighter from WWII. Also, from the Me262A the electrically adjustable stabilizer design was also incorporated. However, the delays due to the redesign meant that production did not commence until after World War II. The XP-86 prototype was rolled out on 8 August 1947 and took its maiden flight occurred on 1 October 1947 with George Welch at the controls. Several people involved with the development of the F-86, including the chief aerodynamicist for the project and one of its other test pilots, claimed that North American test pilot George Welch had unofficially broken the sound barrier in a dive with the XP-86 while on a test flight on 1 October 1947. Although technically rated as subsonic, the Sabre could achieve Supersonic speed in a dive. Chuck Yeager officially broke the sound barrier on October 14, 1947 in the rocket-propelled Bell X-1 during level flight, making it the first true supersonic aircraft. Five years later, on 18 May 1953, Jacqueline Cochran became the first woman to break the sound barrier, flying a "one-off" Canadian-built F-86 Sabre Mk 3, alongside Chuck Yeager. Col. K. K. Compton won the 1951 Bendix air race in an F-86A with an average speed of 553.76 mph.

  The Sabres wing was a compromise; providing excellent straight line speed at all altitudes, but generating poor turning performance at high speed and high altitude. Below 30,000 feet, in thicker air, the Sabre's turning performance improved.

  Various models of the Sabre held world speed records for six consecutive years, setting five official records and winning several National Aircraft Show Bendix Trophies. In September 1948, an F-86A set its first official world speed record of 670 miles per hour, still some 32 miles per hour short of the 702 miles per hour unofficial rocket-powered aircraft speed record. Set with a Me 163B prototype in early July 1944 tests, which itself had a 23.3° wing sweepback angle.

The A mark was bettered in 1952 by an F-86D that flew at 698 mph. The "D" became the first model of a fighter to better its own record, in 1953, with a run of 715 mph. The F-86E and subsequent models incorporated a unique control system, developed by North American, called the "all-flying tail." Where the F-86A contained a booster control system that called for the pilot to do part of the work of controlling the aircraft, the newer system added full power-operated control for better manoeuvrability at high speeds. An "artificial feel" was built into the aircraft's controls to give the pilot forces on the stick that were still conventional, but light enough to enable much better combat control.

Four models of the craft (F-86A, E, F and H) were day fighters or fighter bombers, while the F-86D, K and L versions were all-weather interceptors.

Successive models of the daylight versions - all designed to destroy hostile aircraft in flight or on the ground were equipped with more powerful engines and armament systems. Which ranged from bombs and rockets to machine guns and cannon. All being rated in the 650-mph class with a 600-mile combat radius and a service ceiling of over 45,000 feet. The three interceptor versions sported black radome noses, replacing the so called 'yawning' jet intakes of the other models. The K model, manufactured in Turin, Italy, by Fiat, was flown by NATO forces. The F-86L had added equipment for use in conjunction with the U.S. SAGE (semi-automatic ground environment) defence system. U.S. production of the Sabre Jet ended in December 1956. The F-86 Sabre was also produced under license by Canadair, Ltd as the Canadair Sabre. The final variant of the Canadian Sabre, the Mark 6, is generally rated as having the highest capabilities of any Sabre version made anywhere.

F-86F Specifications

Length: 37 ft 1 in (11.4 m)
Wingspan: 37 ft 0 in (11.3 m)
Height: 14 ft 1 in (4.5 m)

Wing area: 313.4 sq ft (29.11 m²)
Empty weight: 11,125 lb (5,046 kg)
Loaded weight: 15,198 lb (6,894 kg)
Max. takeoff weight: 18,152 lb (8,234 kg)
Powerplant: 1 × General Electric J47-GE-27 turbojet, 5,910 lbf (maximum thrust at 7.950 rpm for five min) with water injection (26.3 kN)
Fuel provisions Internal fuel load: 437 US gallons (1,650 L)), Drop tanks: 2x200 US gallons (760 L) JP-4 fuel

Performance

Maximum speed: 687 mph (1,106 km/h) at sea level at 14,212 lb (6,447 kg) combat weight also reported 678 mph (1,091 km/h) and 599 at 35,000 feet (11,000 m) at 15,352 pounds (6,960 kg). (597 knots (1,106 km/h) at 6446 m, 1,091 and 964 km/h at 6,960 m.)
Stall speed: 124 mph (power off) (108 knots (200 km/h))
Range: 1,525 mi, (2,454 km)
Service ceiling: 49,600 ft at combat weight (15,100 m)
Rate of climb: 9,000 ft/min at sea level (45.72 m/s)
Wing loading: 49.4 lb/ft² (236.7 kg/m²)
lift-to-drag: 15.1
Thrust/weight: 0.38

Armament

Guns: 6 X 0.50 in (12.7 mm) M3 Browning machine guns (1,800 rounds in total)
Rockets: variety of rocket launchers; e.g: 2 Matra rocket pods with 18 SNEB 68 mm rockets per pod
Bombs: 5,300 lb (2,400 kg) of payload on four external hardpoints, bombs were usually mounted on outer two pylons as the inner pairs were plumbed for 2 200 US gallons (760 L) drop tanks which gave the Sabre a more useful range. A wide variety of bombs could be carried (max standard loadout being 2 1,000 lb bombs plus two drop tanks).

CHAPTER ONE

The MiG-15s arrival in Korea, compelled the US Air Force to begin deploying the new F-86 Sabre to Korea. Arriving on scene, the Sabre restored the balance to the air war. In comparison, the F-86 could out dive and out turn the MiG-15, but was inferior in rate of climb, ceiling, and acceleration. Though the Sabre was a more stable gun platform, the MiG-15's all-cannon armament was more effective than the American aircraft's six .50 cal. machine guns. The Sabre's machine guns could fire around 1,200 rounds a minute and had a range of 2,000 feet. Although they were set to converge at 1,200 feet. Each gun had an ammunition canister that could hold 300 rounds, although skilled pilots only filled them with 267 rounds. This was due to stoppages if the canisters were filled, leaving the 'top most' row of bullets empty. In addition, the MiG benefited from the rugged construction typical of Russian aircraft which made it difficult to bring down.

As I neared Sinuiju at 35,000 feet, I could see the snow-covered Manchuria to my right. I pulled the stick back and pushed the throttle fully forward, my Sabre gained some height, before I pushed the stick hard over to perform a quick roll to the left, followed by a gut-wrenching loop, over the MiG-15, desperately trying to escape my attack, but I had him in my sights. Thanks, in large measure to its adjustable horizontal stabilizer, the F-86's flight controls were vastly superior to those on the MiG-15, usually giving us the edge in dogfights.

I hit the fire button on the short, stubby stick with a trigger mechanism to fire the 80 calibre machine guns, and let off a burst of fire which ripped through the tail section of the Mig. This caused flames to shoot out of the tail section along with thick black smoke. The Mig stayed level for a short while before starting to go nose down - into a shallow dive before the dive got steeper and steeper and losing sight of the MiG below the clouds. With no time to reflect, I quickly scanned the sky for any more hostile aircraft, pulling the stick back hard to begin to climb to altitude. I could feel the sweat trickling down my face; feeling both tired and drained. It was not the time to let fatigue take over, as that would be a fatal decision. There were still Migs in the area and they were without a doubt a deadly foe. Getting low on fuel and low on ammunition, meant I needed to head for home in the F-86, the hottest, most lethal fighter the US had at the beginning of 1950. I gave a final glance around me from the bubble canopy to check for any enemy fighters before kicking the rudder pedal left and a slight bank, to put me on the correct heading. The Sabre was without a doubt an awesome aircraft to fly, with a roar almost like thunder from its jet engine. The dials in front of me, still harked back to the warbirds of World War II, but the handling and speed was like going from a push bike to a motorbike.

The lighter MiG-15, however, could operate at higher altitudes than the early Sabres could reach, particularly the F-86As. The Soviets exploited this height advantage consistently. The MiG 15 also had a better rate of climb, could accelerate faster in level flight, and had a tighter turning radius at high altitude. The downside was, it was easy for a MiG pilot to lose control of his plane at high airspeeds. Poor longitudinal stability at high altitudes often led to uncontrollable spins. Some 35 MiG-15s were later claimed by FEAF (Far East Air Forces) to be destroyed solely by uncontrolled spins. The MiG, moreover, had a slow roll rate, and it had an even shorter range than the F-86.

It was not long, before I was on final approach, performing final checks, extending flaps and dropping the tricycle landing gear. I roared over the runway threshold and flared the Sabre slightly as I got to the last few feet, bringing the Sabre down with a slight bump and screech from the tires. I throttled back fully and released the airbrakes before bleeding off enough speed to be able to use the wheel bakes and bring the Sabre down to taxiing speed. A few minutes later, I was on the hard standing with the ground crew rushing around to get me out and the Sabre prepared for her next sortie. I climbed down the cockpit ladder covered in sweat and feeling quite drained.

The Sabre was deployed in response to the Mig threat, with both the P80 and P51 being outclassed by the MiG-15. This realization that the military situation had changed. Gen. Hoyt Vandenberg, the Air Force chief of staff, deployed an F-84E wing and an F-86A wing to Korea. A Strategic Air Command (SAC) unit, the 27th Fighter Escort Wing (FEW), came from Bergstrom AFB (Airforce Base), Texas. The F-84 Thunderjet wing had trained for long-range escort of B-29s and B-50s. However, in Korea it would spend most of its time in the close air support role. The 4th Fighter-Interceptor Wing (FIW), which at the time of the Korean War were flying F86 Sabres. Had its headquartered at Langley AFB, Virginia, had squadrons located at New Castle County Airport, Wilmington, Delaware, at Dover AFB, Delaware, and at Andrews AFB, Maryland. The F86 Sabres were placed in the air superiority role from the start. The move of both the F84 and F86 wings was done in a very short time, due to the demands and nature of the air war after the appearance of the MiG-15.

After being flown to San Diego and McClellan AFB, California, the planes were loaded on an escort carrier in San Diego and a fast tanker in San Francisco. These ships then proceeded to Japan. Due to the hurried nature of the deployment, the aircraft were not properly protected and suffered salt corrosion during their journey. This meant extra time was required to prepare them for combat in the Korean theatre. The intention was to base 4th FIW at Pyongyang and the 27th FEW at Kimpo.

However, the CCF (Chinese Communist Forces) launched a major offensive driving UN troops Southward. This lead to the 27th wing being sent to Taegu.

Due to the crowded conditions at Kimpo, the 4th FIW was directed to send only a detachment of 32 planes.

On December 6, less than a month after being notified it was to move, the 27th FEW flew its first combat mission. Nine days later, on the 15th, the 4th Wing entered combat with an orientation mission over North Korea. Action was not long in coming. This first mission had not gone into the section of northwest Korea soon to become known as "MiG Alley." December 17 saw the 4th FIW F-86 Sabres make their first flight into the area when, the 336th's commander Lieutenant Colonel Bruce Hinton, led a flight of four Sabres up to the

Yalu. Hinton, was hoping he could entice MiGs into combat. The Sabres carried two 120-gallon wing tanks, which gave them an effective combat radius of about 210 miles. However, the round trip between Kimpo and the Yalu was approximately 350 miles. This meant the Sabres needed to keep fuel consumption low by reducing their speed to around 470 mph. This speed, though, was too slow for an effective attack on the fast and agile MiG-15, after initial encounters. This led them to increase speed to around 650 mph.

  A few miles from Sinuiju, four MiG-15s rose to challenge us. The Mig-15s were at times piloted by Soviet pilots, who thought their luck was in with a flight of F-80s. The MiGs were at a tactical disadvantage, still climbing and some 5,000 feet below the flight of Sabres. The Sabres spotted their target and Hinton and his flight dived on the MiGs, dropping their fuel tanks to reduce drag. The MiGs tried to flee, having been taken by complete surprise. They were even more surprised by the speed, by what they still thought were slow F-80s. Hinton looked at his speed and noticed it was well over the 730 mph or Mach 0.95 limit. This high speed meant he was able to quickly get on the tail of a MiG, before letting off a short burst of fire. Rounds impacted on the MiG, causing debris and a stream of fuel to emanate from it. After another couple of bursts flames began to leap out from the fuselage, before the MiG rolled over and dived into the ground. This would become the first Sabre victory over a MiG-15. The downside, was that this short encounter had expended all of his .50 calibre ammunition. Although the weapon had a good rate of fire, it had a short range and lacked punch, especially when compared to the MiG-15s two 23mm cannon and single 37mm cannon.

CHAPTER TWO

We jettisoned the fuel tanks hanging under our wings. Within minutes of crossing over the peninsula, Gucci shouted through the radio. "Ten o'clock low. Five Yak 9s strafing our troops. Engage at will." One by one, we broke formation and began to dive on the Yak 9s below. The Yaks were piston engine fighters from World War Two, which had first flown in 1942. They were no match for a Sabre, the biggest issue for us was that the Yak 9s were quite slow and would mean lowering our speed to a dangerous level. Instead, the best way to attack was with a fast pass, letting off a few rounds, before going around for another run.

I shoved the stick over and rolled into a sharp turn heading down towards the Yak 9s. The Yaks in their day were good aircraft and nearly as good as the P-51. Their only advantage over a Sabre, was their ability to outturn us and try to get in close for a quick burst of fire. As they say 'Speed was life' and never truer than when dogfighting a Yak 9 or a MiG-15 for that matter. As soon as the Yaks spotted us diving they scattered in all directions, knowing they were outclassed. I let off a quick burst onto the Yak I had turned to follow, my bullets hit their target, with a large plume of black smoke belching out of the engine. I pulled the Sabre round in a tight turn, feeling my g suit inflating to counter the high g. As I turned, I found another target just ahead and to my left. I was closing fast, but the sun was partially blocking my view, so with a shot that was more an educated guess than anything else, I let off two bursts of fire, the first missed and the second found their target, taking another Yak out. This time, sending the Yak 9 spiralling into the ground. These Yaks had been an easy target though.

With our fuel levels getting low and just enough to get us back home, we climbed higher and formed up, for the journey home. With 45 minutes we were on final approach to Itazuke. The sight of a friendly runway is always a welcome one, especially in a war zone. Getting wheels on the ground means you are safe, less any unfortunate landing gear collapse or other failure, which is rare to be honest.

Although, it has happened... Slick was returning from patrol on a very dark and wet night, with low cloud cover and a strong gusting wind across the runway. Adding to an already hazardous final approach to Itazuke. The conditions made it far from ideal for an instrument approach. The weather was only just above the minimum to allow flying. As Slick approached a gap in the clouds enabled him to just see the runway lights, battling his way through severe turbulence that felt like the aircraft would shake apart. Slick approached at a slightly higher than normal speed to counter the severe weather. Slick managed to get 'wheels on the ground,' almost as soon as his wheels had touched the ground. Slick's aircraft pulled violently to the left, in doing so the left wheel tore off its hub and the nose slammed down hard on the ground, shearing off the nose wheel strut in the process and causing the Sabre to veer off the rain soaked runway before coming to rest in some vegetation. The Sabre was subsequently written off, but Slick was able to climb out uninjured and was flying on operations the very next day.

I looked out of the cockpit scanning the sky for enemy, you continuously moved your head scanning every inch of sky. Then I just made out the contrails of four MiGs about 10,000 feet above our flight. Quickly passing the contact over the radio to the rest of my flight, "Four MiGs above us at 2 o'clock." Low on fuel, we had very little time for any encounter. The best option was to try and avoid them, the hope was they would stand off and observe, as was their new practice, only mixing it up when they had two. With their bases just minutes away from the combat arena, the MiG-15s usually held the altitude advantage and thus could choose the time and position of their attacks. The mission of the MiG-15s was to guard the vital bridges spanning the Yalu River along with the Supung hydro-electric powerplant and various airbases between Yalu and Pyongyang by stopping B-29 and B-26 bombers reaching their target. Although, when not offering close air support, strike missions and airfield attack, Sabre's would fly into MiG alley to entice MiGs up for a fight. MiG alley was located in the North Western corner of North Korea along the Yalu River and stretched slightly into Manchuria or now, usually refered to as Northeast China, where most of the air battles between F-86s and MiG-15s took place.

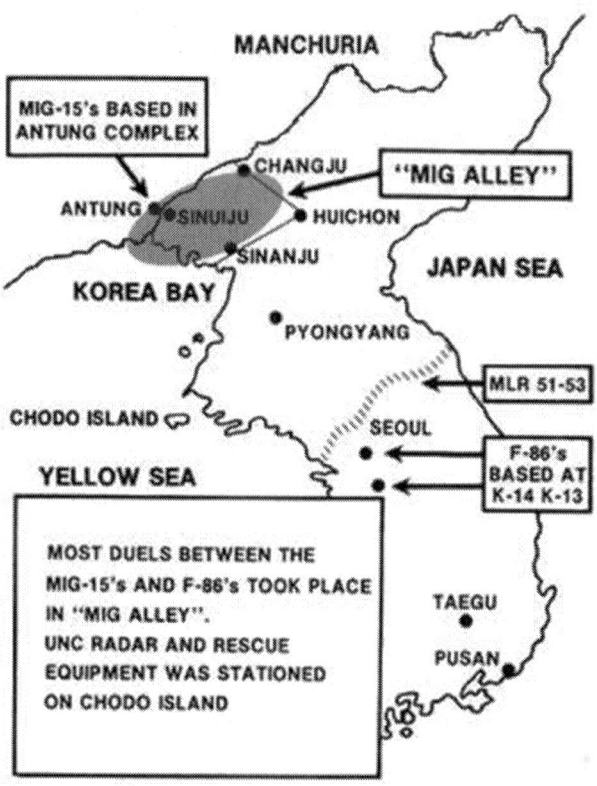

For whatever reason the MiGs stayed above us and we could safely fly out of the area. If they had attacked, they would have had the advantage of speed and height along with our low fuel, we may have got a few rounds off, before having to make a run for it and the twenty-minute flight home

After landing, we taxied in pairs to our ramp in front of the fighter hangars. Ground crew ran out and quickly leapt all over our aircraft almost before we had shut the engines down. I gave a cursory glance over my aircraft and saw a couple bullet holes just in front of my tail. I climbed and walked away from the ramp which is a dangerous place to be with fuel, bullets and bombs. Accidents on the ramp were more common than they should be. They ranged from decapitation by propellers, being sucked into jet intakes or blown over by the jet blast from an aircraft. One such story outside of Korea, was of a navigator instructor who, crossing the apron wearing his 'bone dome' to protect him from the severe cold following heavy snowfall, was unaware of the snow blower, which went on to swallow him whole. He luckily survived minus one ear.

CHAPTER THREE

The MiG hit 550 mph, he pulled back and screamed almost straight up. Right on his tail, I felt the tight squeeze of the air bladders of the G suit on my legs as the forces of five times gravity pulled at my insides. I felt the vibrations of his slip stream along with feeling my Sabre shake as it climbed up and up. At 47,000 feet, my controls became sloppy as my F-86 strained in the thin air to make the final 2,000 feet, the maximum altitude possible for control. My concentration grew as I topped out at 48,000, unable to keep climbing due to the turbulence from the MiG. I levelled off, I watched and guessed the MiG had hit at least 50,000 feet. The MiG must be nearing a stall and I waited for him to start is decent back down. As the MiG began its descent back down, the pilot had made a fatal error and allowed the MiG to stall sending it into an uncontrollable spin. Another MiG pilot had fallen to the MiGs horizontal instability and the ease at which a MiG-15 could be got into a spin. I watched the MiG spiral downwards before seeing it, impact and explode on the ground thousands of feet below me.

During the first four months of 1953, 24 MiGs was seen to enter spins. Half of these were assessed as accidental, and 11 fighters crashed. These losses represented more than 12 percent of the MiGs destroyed in that period. Several examples of the MiG-15's propensity to spin occurred on just one day. During both morning and afternoon engagements on May 19, 1953, 41 Sabres met 48 MiG-15s. In the first encounter, a pair of Sabre's, callsign Cobra 3 and 4 were flying at 45,000 feet when four enemy fighters jumped them. One MiG pulled in too tight on Cobra 3 and began to spin. The pilot ejected at 41,000 feet. Shortly afterward, another MiG overshot Cobra 4 and vanished. Looking over his shoulder for further attackers, Cobra 4 saw another MiG in a spin at 45,000 feet. Five minutes later, another pair of Sabres callsign Python 1 and 2 were jumped by eight MiGs. Python 1 got on the tail of a MiG shooting at his wingman and scored hits on the enemy's left wing and tail section. The MiG began to turn right, then, suddenly, snapped to the left and began to spin from 34,000 feet. Its corkscrew continued all the way to the ground. The morning action was not over. About 30 minutes after the second event - four MiGs bounced a flight of Sabres at 42,000 feet. The MiGs, however, overshot their quarry and quickly became the hunted. Callsign Boxer 1 let off several bursts of fire, into the left side of the fuselage of one of the MiGs. The fighter began spinning, and its pilot ejected at 35,000 feet. Then in the afternoon, two MiGs attacked Python 5 and 6 at 43,000 feet. A scissoring duel quickly ensued, and Python 6 managed to score some hits, causing the MiG burst into flames, which then caused the MiG to enter a tight and unrecoverable tight spin.

After the end of World War II, the Soviet Union captured a wealth of German jet engine and aeronautical research. Utilizing this, they produced their first practical jet fighter, the MiG-9, in early 1946. While capable, this aircraft lacked the top speed of the standard American jets of the day, such as the P-80 Shooting Star. Though the MiG-9 was operational, Russian designers continued to have issues perfecting the German HeS-011 axial-flow jet engine. As a result, airframe designs produced by Artem Mikoyan and Mikhail Gurevich's design bureau began to outpace the ability to produce engines to power them.

While the Soviets struggled with developing jet engines, the British had created advanced centrifugal flow engines that were also reliable for a jet engine of the time. In 1946, Soviet aviation minister Mikhail Khrunichev and aircraft designer Alexander Yakovlev approached Premier Joseph Stalin with the suggestion of buying several British jet engines to aid in their own research and development. Stalin believed the British would not part with their advanced technology. However, Stalin still gave them permission to contact London. In a surprising twist of fate, the British agreed to sell the Soviets several several Rolls-Royce Nene engines along with a licensing agreement for overseas production. Once the engines arrived in the Soviet Union, engine designer Vladimir Klimov, began the process of reverse engineering them. This process resulted in the RD-45, which effectively resolved the engine issue for the MiG-9.

With a good jet engine in production the Council of Ministers, issued decree #493-192 on April 15, 1947, calling for two prototypes for a new jet fighter. The time allowed for test flights was a matter of months. With the tight schedule, MiG decided to use the MiG-9 as a basis and modify it, with swept wings and a redesigned tail. For the test flights it was designated the I-310. The I-310 was capable of speeds of up to 650mph and defeated the Lavochkin La-168. The LA-168 was similar in design to the I-310. Although, the LA-168 had shoulder mounted, swept wings and a t-tail. Lavochkin then went on to produce the A-174, a 0.9 scale version of the A-168 and fitted with a Rolls Royce Derwent engine.

The I-310 was Re-designated the MiG-15, the first production aircraft flew December 31, 1948, before entering service in 1949. The MiG-15s principle role was to intercept American bombers of the time, such as the B-29 Superfortress. To undertake this role, he MiG-15 was equipped with two 23mm cannons and a 37 mm cannon.

The first upgrade to the MiG-15 came in 1950, with the arrival of the MiG-15bis. While the aircraft contained numerous minor improvements, it also possessed the new Klimov VK-1 engine and external hardpoints for rockets and bombs. Widely exported, the Soviet Union provided the new aircraft to the People's Republic of China. First seeing combat at the end of the Chinese Civil War, the MiG-15 was flown by Soviet pilots from the 50th IAD. The MiG-15 scored its first kill on 28 April 1950, when one downed a Nationalist Chinese P-38 Lightning.

With the outbreak of the Korean War in June 1950, the North Koreans began operations flying a variety of piston-engine fighters. These were soon swept from the sky by American jets and B-29 formations began a systematic aerial campaign against the North Koreans. With the Chinese entry into the conflict, the MiG-15 began to appear in the skies over Korea. Quickly proving superior to straight-wing American jets such as the F-80 and F-84 Thunderjet, the MiG-15 temporarily gave the Chinese the advantage in the air and ultimately forced United Nations forces to halt daylight bombing. The most famous engagements for the MiG-15 were those involving the F-86 occurred over northwestern North Korea in an area known as "MiG

Alley."" In this area, Sabres and MiGs frequently dueled, making it the birthplace of jet vs. jet aerial combat.

Eager to inspect the MiG-15, the United States offered a bounty of $100,000 to any enemy pilot who defected with an aircraft. This offer was taken up by Lieutenant No Kum-Sok, who defected on November 21, 1953. At the end of the war, the US Air Force claimed a kill ratio of around 10 to 1 for MiG-Sabre battles. Although this ratio in some circles is believed to be lower. In the years after the Korean War, the MiG-15 equipped many of the Soviet Union's Warsaw Pact allies as well as numerous other countries around the world.

Several MiG-15s flew with the Egyptian Air Force during the 1956 Suez Crisis, though their pilots were routinely beaten by the Israelis. The MiG-15 also saw extended service with the People's Republic of China under the designation J-2. These Chinese MiGs frequently skirmished with Republic of China aircraft around the Straits of Taiwan during the 1950s. Largely replaced in Soviet service by the MiG-17, the MiG-15 remained in many countries' arsenals into the 1970s. Trainer versions of the aircraft continued to fly for another twenty to thirty years with some nations. A true testament to the design, even if it was British and later American technology that shaped it into a formidable 1950s fighter.

The F-86 and the MiG-15 were very close in performance, though throughout the Korean War the MiG had an edge in altitude and armament. The Sabre, however, was a much more agile and faster aircraft. The Americans also used superior tactics with greater flexibility and enjoyed a higher standard of training. This superiority showed in the air battles fought in MiG Alley. Interestingly, the majority of the Sabre aces (68 percent) were over 28 years old, supposedly "old men" for jet fighter combat. Conversely, 67 percent of those fliers who had no kills were less than 25 years old. Nearly 38 percent of the 810 F-86 kills (305.5) were made by the 39 Sabre aces. These victories were achieved at great effort and at a cost. FEAF lost 1,466 aircraft, including 139 planes in air-to-air combat. Seventy-eight of the latter losses were Sabres. The command also suffered 1,144 dead and 306 wounded officers and airmen during aerial operations. Given that FEAF was never a large organization, it nevertheless accomplished a great deal. Of the 1,040,708 sorties flown by the UN air forces in the war, almost two-thirds (720,980) were flown by FEAF aircraft. Miscellaneous sorties, which included such varied missions as reconnaissance and training, constituted the greatest number of sorties, with 222,078. Interdiction followed with 192,581 sorties, and cargo with 181,659 sorties. Falling well below these numbers were close air support missions, with 57,665 sorties, and counterair/ air superiority missions, with 66,997. Thus, the air superiority missions constituted only 9 percent of the total FEAF sorties of the war. This small percentage belies the importance of the air superiority mission, for without air superiority, the success of the ground campaign becomes problematic.

CHAPTER FOUR

Although their .50-caliber machine guns damaged a number of MiGs, the Americans complained that their armament did not have enough stopping power to consistently bring down the MiGs. These high-speed, G-pulling fights allowed little chance for deflection shooting. The only sure way to make a kill was to get behind a MiG and "fly up his tailpipe" to pepper the jet from close range. Again, in the type of fast paced combat with the relative speeds of jet aircraft, this often meant getting just one chance to shoot and one chance to kill. Due to this, Sabre pilots began asking for heavier armament. Such weapons would eventually be delivered, but only as a test and with mixed results, the Sabre would spend its career with the same armament. As 1951 opened, however, the 4th FIG, like many other Air Force units in Korea, had more pressing concerns than armament. The Chinese offensive, which had been launched in late November, was now in full swing, and the UN forces were in a precipitous flight. Pyongyang, where the 8th and 18th FBGs had begun operating in just the last weeks of November, was evacuated on December 3. Seoul's turn came a month later. Hardly settled into its new base at Kimpo, the 4th FIG was ordered to evacuate, and quickly. The last Sabre flew back to Japan on January 2. That evening, as gunfire erupted around the field, the remaining pilots and ground crews flew out in a C-54. Also evacuating Kimpo were the F-80C-equipped 51st FIW and the 67th TRS with its RF-51Ds. Most of the 51st's planes had flown out earlier, but a couple still remained on the 3d, when they made one last strike before flying to safety. Despite the closeness of the enemy, a C-119 made a final, very dangerous trip into Kimpo early on the 4th to pick up any remaining personnel. Later that day, Seoul fell. The Communist offensive finally ground to a halt roughly along the 37th Parallel. In late January, Lt. Gen. Matthew B. Ridgway, the new Eighth Army commander (who succeeded Gen. Walker after his death in a traffic accident), ordered a reconnaissance in force while the CCF and North Koreans regrouped. This "limited" offensive quickly turned into a full-blown drive. By April 9, Seoul had been retaken for the last time, and the UN forces continued to press forward. A renewed offensive by the Chinese Army failed, and by July the battlefront had settled down to a line winding from below Kaesong on the west to above Kansong on the shore of the Sea of Japan. For the rest of the war all ground action, reminiscent of the positional and bloody trench warfare of World War I, would occur along this line. The MiGs were little seen during the CCF advance in December to January. Stalin had prohibited his pilots from providing air cover for the Chinese, and they apparently spent much of their time in training. Additionally, great effort was expended with scant success during this period in attempting to rehabilitate a number of North Korean airfields for use by the MiGs. However, the Chinese took this opportunity to move at least ten MiG-15s of their 4th Air Division to Antung to gain combat experience. Accompanied by Soviet fliers, the Chinese flew their first missions on December 28. The Communist fliers, apparently figuring that with the removal of the Sabres and Thunderjets to Japan, their only opponents would be the F-80s and F-51s, became bolder and began appearing farther south. On January 21, four 49th FBG Shooting Stars escorting an RF-80 south of Sinuiju were attacked by 12 MiGs. The F-80s were unable to protect the reconnaissance plane and lost one of their number also. That same day, however, this new found aggressiveness cost the enemy. Two F-84E flights were bombing a bridge over the Chongchon River when they were jumped by 16 Chinese-flown MiGs. In this first fight between the Chinese and the Americans, the Americans lost one plane, but Lt. Col. William E. Bertram, the 523d FBS commander, got behind a MiG and with some well-placed shots knocked the enemy fighter out of the air. With his victory, Bertram became the first Thunderjet pilot to score a MiG kill. The Chinese had now been blooded in aerial combat over Korea, but it was accidents, not combat, that proved the most costly to them, during their initial two-month tour at Antung. They experienced a serious accident for every 42.2 sorties, and it quickly became evident to both the Chinese and the Soviets that the Chinese needed much more training. The 4th Air Division was withdrawn from combat operations, and for the next six months the

Soviets were responsible for all air operations in MiG Alley. Detachments of the 4th FIW and the 27th FEW had been ordered back to Korea on January 14, this time to Taegu. Still far removed from the Yalu, instead of operating in the air superiority role, the Sabres were given air-to-ground bombing missions. Close air support was not the F-86A's forte, but the 4th flew more than 150 sorties before returning to its proper mission. Although the straight-wing F-84Es were underpowered and no match for the MiG-15s, the 27th's Thunder-jets marked their return to Korea in spectacular fashion. It had become apparent to the FEAF and Fifth Air Force commanders that the Communists were expending great effort to repair their airfields at Pyongyang and around Sinuiju. The latter field was already well-covered with anti-aircraft batteries on both sides of the Yalu; now Pyongyang experienced a phenomenal growth in the number of antiaircraft guns. If these defensive efforts succeeded, the complexion of the air war would change dramatically. To thwart the enemy, Gen. Stratemeyer ordered a B-29 strike on Pyongyang on January 23. Forty F-80s of the 49th FBG would fly flak suppression missions prior to the B-29 attack. Another strike was also planned for the 23d. Colonel Ashley B. Packard, the 27th FEW's commander, proposed sending eight flights of F-84s to strafe Sinuiju. Two flights would make up the attack package while the remaining aircraft would act as top cover. Both missions on the 23d were executed without fault. The flak suppression F-80s at Pyongyang did their job so well that the B-29s drew little fire as they placed 90 percent of their bombs on the airfield. At Sinuiju, it was MiGs, not flak, which met the attackers. Eight aircraft had already made their runs across the airfield before the enemy reacted. Dust clouds on the Antung gave a warning that MiGs were taking off. Because they took off so late into the attack, the MiGs were unable to gain an altitude advantage, and most of the fighting was done below 20,000 feet. For almost 30 minutes, a fierce air battle raged over Sinuiju. First Lieutenant Jacob Kratt, Jr., scored a double kill in less than two minutes, and Capts. Allen McGuire and William W. Slaughter each claimed a MiG. The 27th pilots went on to claim four MiGs destroyed, three probable's, and four damaged against no losses.

Three days after this battle, Kratt downed a Yak-3 for his final victory of the war. At this time there was still some concern at some command levels about the success of Gen. Ridgway's new offensive. Until such success could be assured, Gen. Partridge ordered many of his units, including the 49th FBW, the 27th FEW, and the 4th FIW, again back to Japan. Soon it became evident that the enemy was falling back, and the Sabres of the 334th FIS were again ordered forward to Korea. With many of the Yalu bridges still relatively undamaged, FEAF directed more B-29 strikes against these structures. Because of the threat of the MiGs, but more importantly because of the urgent need of their services against other targets during the Chinese offensive, the B-29s had not ventured into MiG Alley for some time. Unescorted B-29s operating in the area were often met by MiGs. As the ground fighting damped down, FEAF decided that it was time to return to northwest Korea, regardless of the enemy jets. On March 1, 98th BG (Bombardment Group) B-29s bombed a bridge near Chongju. Although scheduled to be escorted by F-80s, strong headwinds prevented a rendezvous, and the 18 Superfortresses proceeded alone. Shortly after coming off the target, the bombers were attacked by nine MiGs. A desperate fight by the B-29 gunners ensued, who shot down one of the fighters, but ten of the bombers were damaged, three severely. If this kind of damage continued, the B-29s would not be able to operate over northwest Korea. When Gen. Partridge recalled elements of the 4th FIG back to Korea, the 334th FIS moved to Suwon. At this time, Suwon was just a mudhole with a single runway and no taxiway. Planes had to taxi back up the runway to reach their parking areas, naturally delaying other landings. Facilities at the base were primitive, but the field would have to do for the time because it was the closest one to MiG Alley. Also, the 336th FIS moved to Taegu and staged its Sabres through Suwon. On March 12, four 36th FBS Shooting Stars on an armed reconnaissance mission near Namsi were jumped by 12 MiGs. The F-80 pilots scored some hits on the enemy planes but did not bring down any. During the battle, however, two of the MiGs collided and exploded. These enemy pilots may have been new to combat, for their shooting was extremely poor. Five days later, near Sunchon, another trio of 36th FBS planes encountered more MiGs. During a low-level fight in and out of clouds, a MiG collided with 1st Lt. Howard J. Landry's F-80. Landry was posthumously credited with downing the enemy fighter. The Soviet pilots may have demonstrated poor gunnery because they were in the process of changing units.

   These new pilots were more carefully chosen than their predecessors, this policy though, had the effect of having everyone learn everything all over again. Although their aerial activity declined somewhat, MiG losses climbed as the newcomers met veteran American pilots. In late March, the Sabres and MiGs fought a couple of inconclusive battles as the Communists seemed unwilling to mix it up. Actions on April 3 and 4, however, showed the enemy airmen to be more determined. This new aggressiveness did not prevent them from losing three aircraft on the 3d and another on the 4th against no Sabre losses. One of the victors on April 3 was Capt. Jabara, who claimed the first of his long string of MiG kills. A week later, Jabara would bag his second MiG. Reacting to pressure from Gen. Curtis E. LeMay, the SAC commander, who wanted to see his Thunderjets operating in their regular role as escort fighters rather than in ground attack, Gen. Stratemeyer assigned the 27th FEW F-84Es to accompany the B-29s on their next couple of forays into MiG Alley. Taking off from cloud-covered Itazuke on April 7, 48 F-84s met the bombers on time and spread out alongside the B-29s as they bombed bridges at Sinuiju and Uiju. Overhead, Sabres provided high cover. Near the target, 30 MiGs slanted down through the F-86s for an attack on the bombers. Only one made it through the wall of F-84s, but this one was able to down a B-29. A follow-up attack on the Sinuiju Bridge on the 12th proved more deadly to the bombers. Instead of flying in a compact formation, the bombers were spaced too far apart, forcing the 54 escorting F-84s to thin their ranks. About 50 MiGs swarmed over the B-29s like angry wasps as they approached the target, sending down two in flames and damaging another so severely that it barely made Suwon. Four others were also damaged. B-29 gunners claimed ten MiGs, of which seven were later credited during another ferocious aerial encounter between B-29s and MiGs. Two were kills made by Sgt. Billy G. Beach. The faster enemy jets disseminated the straggling formations before the F-84s could react, although the Thunderjet pilots did claim three fighters as probably destroyed. Unlike the previous mission, when they were unable to do much to counter the attack, the Sabres were very active. At times, the Sabre pilots pursued their quarry through the bomber formations, being shot at by gunners and F-84s alike. Colonel Meyer and Lt. Col. Hinton each scored their last victories of the war, while Capt. Jabara added one more MiG to his scorecard. Also downing an enemy jet was Capt. Howard M. Lane. The loss of the three B-29s, coupled with the damages sustained by other bombers, was a blow to FEAF and FEAF Bomber Command. With fewer than 100 B-29s assigned, such losses could not be tolerated. Reluctantly, Stratemeyer called a temporary halt to B-29 attacks in the Sinuiju area. Just as reluctantly, the FEAF commander radioed LeMay that Partridge was reporting that the Thunder-jets were outclassed by the MiGs and that the Korea-based F-86s were better suited for counterair and escort missions. Only when fields and facilities in Korea were ready for them would the 27th's F-84s be utilized again in the escort role. In these latest fights, the U.S. fliers noted a growing proficiency on the part of their foes. Unit cohesion in formations of up to 16 aircraft appeared to be much better, and the enemy pilots exhibited greater aggressiveness.

This cohesiveness was displayed in battles on April 16 and 18 when neither side was able to gain an advantage. The Communists' new found competence worried FEAF, especially since reconnaissance missions showed that they were busily rehabilitating airfields in North Korea and that some of these fields might soon be ready to receive MiGs. Beginning April 17, FEAF launched a major effort to halt the enemy's work by sending its B-29s against the airfields. Again, the Sabres of the 4th FIW were in the air to protect the bombers.

Responding to the new threat presented by the MiGs, the 4th's pilot's devised new tactics. They were helped in this due to the fact that the facilities at Suwon had been improved and both squadrons, the 334th and the 336th, could now be based there. With both squadrons at Suwon, more F-86s could be dispatched to the Yalu, of particular importance since the MiGs often attacked in large numbers. Instead of four aircraft, the number of Sabres in a flight was increased to six. In this size formation the F-86s could counter the usual MiG tactic of splitting a four-ship flight into two pairs, one climbing and one diving. Four of the Sabres would go after the climbers while the remaining two F-86s would chase the divers. The 4th also began scheduling their patrols to operate more closely.

These new tactics received their first test on April 22. That afternoon, 12 Sabres, sporting the black and white fuselage and wing stripes that identified the 4th FIW, were just finishing an uneventful patrol when they were jumped by 36 MiGs. The MiGs themselves were attacked by 12 more F-86s which had just arrived to relieve the first patrol. Four of the enemy planes were downed in the ensuing dogfight, along with four more damaged. Among those scoring were Lt. Col. Eagleston, who got his second, and final, victory of the war, and Capt. Jabara. This was Jabara's fourth kill, making him the leader in aerial victories. Although Jabara was scheduled to rotate back to Japan with the 334th FIS, because he was close to achieving "ace" status, he was allowed to stay and fly with the 335th FIS which replaced his squadron at Suwon. Victories, however, would be hard to achieve for the next month, with only one attained until May 20. Although the North Koreans doggedly continued to work on the airfields, methodical B-29 raids and night intruder attacks by B-26s prevented them from fully repairing their fields. Watched constantly, the airfields were never used effectively. The field at Sinuiju proved more of a problem; surrounded by numerous antiaircraft guns, it was also protected by MiGs based just across the river at Antung. When the Communists began intensive construction and repair work to the field in early May, Gen. Partridge decided it was time to revisit "Sunny Joe." On the afternoon of May 9, while F-80s, F-51s, and Marine F4Us pounded the airfield, Air Force F-86s and F-84s and Navy F9Fs covered the attackers. Approximately 50 MiG-15s rose from Antung, but only a handful made half-hearted passes on the attackers, and minimal damage was inflicted on either side. At one point, a Sabre flight was paced, but not attacked by eight MiGs flying only a few hundred yards away, just across the river. Grievously damaged, Sinuiju was out of action for the time being. Activity in MiG Alley slackened for the next couple of weeks until, on May 20, some 50 enemy jets engaged several flights of Sabre's. A call for help brought more Sabres to the scene. In the thick of the action was Capt. Jabara. Despite the handicap of being unable to drop one of his wing tanks, which greatly affected his plane's handling, Jabara remained in the fight. This will, was rewarded with two more kills, bringing his score to six and making him the first jet ace in history.

Another MiG fell to F-86 guns, one was claimed a probable, and five were damaged. After this poor showing, the enemy fighters vanished for more than a week. They showed up again on the 31st, when they tried to down a couple of B-29s s South of Sinuiju. Their attempt was unsuccessful. A B-29 gunner got one of the attackers, and Sabres shot down two more. The Soviet pilots were a bit more successful the following day. One B-29 went down in flames, but other gunners destroyed two MiGs, and an F-86 got a third. That same day a Navy exchange pilot flying with the 336th FIS also downed a MiG-15.

CHAPTER FIVE

The stage was set for a major effort in June 1951, one in which the Soviets attempted to obtain air superiority over the Chinese supply lines to support Peng's planned "sixth phase offensive". Realizing that the CPVA could not overwhelm the UNC forces with manpower alone, the aim of this phase was to recover DPRK territory north of the 38th Parallel that had been lost to the UNC's spring counter offensives. Peng's previous campaign ended prematurely on May 20, having been defeated, according to his personal report to Mao, by ravaging UNC air attacks on his logistics system. Only 60-70% of the supplies required, including, food, water, clothing, ammunition and other equipment had managed to reach frontline troops. The Chinese were desperate for increased air cover over their supply lines from the Yalu to Pyongyang, the 64th IAK challenged the 4th FIG repeatedly during the third week of June. By this time the combat experience of the Soviet pilots began to show improved combat proficiency along with an increased aggressiveness in the way they fought. Their tactics had improved and were much more of a formidable foe. This led to a belief by Sabre pilot's intelligence that the covering fighters were Russian instructors directing Chinese students and began referring to the para as "honchos" which is Japanese for "Boss." The red-nosed MiGs of the 324th IAD were particularly visible. This made the USAF believe these were the personal markings of one or two senior Russian instructors, the covering flight leader was frequently called "Casey Jones" after an American railroader who died tragically when his passenger train, the Cannonball Express, collided with a stalled freight train at Vaughan. He gained hero status for the way he tried to prevent the train crash and save lives.

His wide-flying wingman was rarely seen, leading the Americans to believe that "Casey Jones" primarily operated solo. "Casey Jones'" view of Lt Col Glenn Eagleston's Sabre. According to the 336th FIS "Rocketeers" CO, Lt Col Bruce Hinton (who had scored the first MiG kill of the Korean War). "Ol' Casey, also known as 'Honcho', was an exceptional pilot. His normal procedure was to sit up high all by himself, then dive down at a very high rate and attack any F-86 that seemed isolated and alone. He was easily spotted in the air due to his MiGs significant paint job, with a red nose and fuselage stripes". On 17 June, in the first battle of this series, "Casey Jones" turned out to be Capt Sergei Kramarenko. On his second mission that day the Soviet pilot led a flight of six MiG-15bis that had been sent aloft to intercept a dozen Sabres flying in two formations.

This first clash, proved nothing, with Kramarenko ducking into a cloud cover to escape being "sandwiched" between the Sabres' main group and the top cover four-ship. Turning and climbing back out of the clouds, Kramarenko found himself alone, above and behind the Sabres' covering flight. As Kramarenko later recalled, "Now, below me, there were these three Sabres, which were looking for me below them. Without losing not even a second, I jumped them. Now it was my turn to attack, but somehow they spotted me and immediately they split – the wingmen performed a diving turn to the left, and the leader a climbing right turn. This tactic was a trap, for whichever one I attacked, I would be forced to turn my tail to the others and then they would attack me from a strong firing position. I had no choice but to decide fast. Who shall I attack? Should I attack the pair which was diving, or the Sabre which was climbing? If I jumped the first ones, the latter would dive after me and he would shoot me down. That's why I choose the latter. So, I dived and soon I put myself behind him. I aimed, and at a distance of about 1,970ft I opened up.

To slow down and hold my fire until I was closer to the Sabres was impossible, because the two remaining jets could catch me. My shells struck the Sabre. Evidently, some of the projectiles hit it close to the engine, because the aircraft began to leave a trail of dark grey smoke. The Sabre began to descend, and later entered into a steep dive. I did not see my victim fall, because when I looked back, I saw a couple of Sabres at 500m. I immediately reversed my heading, passed over the Sabres and dived to the right towards the Suiho Dam hydro-electric station on the Yalu River. I hoped that the gunners of the dams AA batteries would help me to get these Sabres off of my tail. And that was what happened. During the course of this engagement, Lt Col Hinton had spotted the Sabre of Lt Col Glenn Eagleston (an 18.5-victory World War II ace who was now CO of the 334th FIS). "About 500ft behind him was a MiG with a red nose and stripes on his fuselage. 'Casey Jones!' And he was pounding the Sabre with cannon fire. I could see the MiG fire, and see its shells hitting the Sabre, with flame and sparks marking the strikes on the fuselage". Hinton's account correlates well with Kramarenko's, ending with "the MiG suddenly broke away and dove toward the Yalu, easily pulling away from me. I broke off and looked for the stricken F-86. I found him sort of floating at about 20,000ft. The fires had gone out, but he had some big holes in the fuselage. I tried talking to him, but his radio had been hit by another cannon shell. We were flying at about 0.7 Mach, and he was steadily losing altitude. It took forever, but we finally made it to friendly territory. I called Suwon tower, informing them that I was bringing in a cripple, and to clear the runway and alert the meat wagon and fire trucks. He was going to have to make a wheels-up landing as the MiG had shot out all the controls". Following the successful belly landing, the Sabre's riddled hulk was cannibalized for parts and used as a decoy at the end of the runway – although DBR on June 17, F-86A-5 49-1281 was not written off for a further eight days.

The June air battles continued throughout the week, and although the challenge to the Sabres' superiority was in question, it was met effectively, although with increased losses. The 64th IAK suffered seven MiG-15s destroyed and four pilots killed, while the 4th FIG lost four Sabres (including Eagleston's) and three pilots killed. Despite these successes, the Communists realized that Belov's two MiG divisions had not managed to gain air superiority from the Sabres. Stalin was unwilling to commit any more Soviet fighter units to the contest, urged Mao to send "at least eight fighter aviation divisions" into combat, and provided 372 MiG-15s to replace the MiG-9s in six PLAAF FADs to do so. He emphasised that "it is necessary for the Chinese to rely only on their own aviation at the front". The PLAAF promised to have these forces ready for battle in November. Meanwhile, Peng cancelled his "sixth phase offensive".

The summer monsoon season blanketed Korea in bad weather – cloud bases at about 2,000ft, layered up to 32,500ft most days – with morning fog and incessant rain effectively grounding the 64th IAK and limiting all-jet combat to just six engagements. The 4th FIG continued to dominate the air, destroying ten MiGs and killing four pilots for only two combat losses. Early in this period the 4th FIG was reinforced with the arrival of 30 more F-86A-5s and 45 new F-86E-5s. This was in part to replace the 17 Sabres that had been lost to accident and combat loss. Along with aircraft, was a large cache of spare parts. Along with the new F-86s came fresh, eager and experienced fighter pilots to buoy up the ranks. These were led by the flamboyant Col Francis S. Gabreski, the third-ranking and top living USAAF ace from World War II with 28 victories over the Luftwaffe. "Gabby" Gabreski was the commander of the 56th FIG at Selfridge AFB until he was named as the 4th FIW's deputy commander, and he sailed to Korea with a group of 56th FIG pilots he had hand-picked to accompany him back into battle. "Gabby" scored his first MiG kill on July 8. The highest-scoring surviving USAAF ace of World War II, Col "Gabby" Gabreski (right) returned to combat in the summer of 1951 and got his second MiG kill on September 2 that year. One week later he congratulated the USAF's second and third jet aces, 1Lts Dick Becker and Ralph "Hoot" Gibson.

Improved weather conditions in September allowed RF-80 photo-reconnaissance missions to resume, and FEAF Intelligence was surprised to find that the Communists had taken advantage of the weather-related reprieve to begin building three new airfields in North Korea. Halfway between the Yalu and Pyongyang, a clutch of three air bases – Namsi, Taechon and Saamcham – were rapidly being completed, and FEAF Bomber Command hurried to destroy them. Once again, the MiG-15 proved its mettle as a bomber destroyer. On October 23, nine B-29s (of the 307th BG) headed for Namsi airfield, escorted by 55 F-84s (49th and 136th FBGs) and screened by 34 Sabres. The 303rd IAD's three regiments scrambled 58 MiG-15bis, followed 15 minutes later by 26 from the 324th IAD's two regiments. The 18th GvIAP led the assault, with two squadrons engaging the Sabres and the third attacking the bombers. The MiGs shot down three B-29s and badly damaged five others, two of which made emergency landings at Kimpo and were later "transferred to depot for disposition."

In spite of claims from bomber gunners, Thunderjets and Sabres, no MiGs were lost, and only three were damaged in the battle. After losing eight bombers with five damaged, FEAF HQ ordered that daytime bomber operations be discontinued from October 28. This was a tacit admission that the Fifth Air Force had failed to achieve air superiority north of the Chongchon River sufficient to allow the B-29s to do their job, and that these ponderously slow World War II bombers were not survivable against modern swept-wing jet interceptors. This victory came at some cost to the Communists, however, as eight MiG-15bis and three pilots had been lost to Sabres during this period. On October 22, 1951, the MiG-15 once again proved deadly as a bomber destroyer when three of them mortally damaged one of nine B-29s targeting Taechon airfield. Seen here from one of the other Superfortresses in the formation, the jets are peeling away following their firing passes. The greatest victory for the MiG-15 during the Korean War, came on October 23, 1951 when 84 MiGs engaged 34 F-86s and 55 F-84s to get to nine B-29s approaching Namsi airfield. Three bombers were destroyed and two more DBR. By the end of the month FEAF HQ had discontinued daylight operations by the slow and vulnerable World War II-era Superfortresses. In November the 64th IAK was joined by two PLAAF and one KPAF MiG-15 divisions, organized into what was called the "1st United Air Army" (or OVA by the Soviets) and commanded by Chinese Gen Liu Zhen. This brought the total number of MiGs in the theatre, to 525, of which 290 were based in the Andong area once Takushan airfield. Takushan was a 7,000ft concrete runway ideal for jets, 50 miles down the coast west of Andong. The rest other extra MiGs were stationed at the more distant Manchurian bases, except for the KPAF's 1st FAD, which deployed 26 MiG-15s to Uiju, in North Korea, on November 7. Control of these increased forces was fractured since neither Mao nor Stalin would allow their units to be under the authority of the other. Consequently, while a separate OVA/KP (command post) was established only 60 yards from the 64th IAK/KP at Andong, coordination consisted only of the OVA HQ passing information to the Soviets so that the latter could time their launches to cover the withdrawal and return of Chinese and Korean fighters. The PLAAF's 4th FAD, formed from the cadre of pilots trained by the 29th GvIAP in 1950, quickly became the most experienced Chinese MiG-15 unit.

Responding to the MiG build-up in Manchuria and grievous losses to the B-29 force, HQ USAF dispatched 75 new F-86Es to Korea – enough to replace the 4th FIG's F-86A losses and establish a second unit, the 51st FIG, at Suwon. Compared with the first transoceanic shipment, this one was much better organized, as attested by the tidy parking arrangements aboard Cape Esperance.

The introduction of PLAAF and KPAF units to the war more than compensated numerically for the departure of the V-VS's 151st GvIAD, which had completed its year-long mission and returned to the USSR. The MiGs being passed on to the KPAF. At the same time Gen Belov also departed, turning command over to Lt Gen Lobov, another World War II veteran and ace.

As more MiG-15s arrived in theatre, Sabre numbers grew to match the increased threat. The day of the slaughter of the FEAF B-29s over Namsi – known as "Black Tuesday" – Gen Vandenberg ordered that 75 more F-86E-1s, hastily gathered from various Air Defence Command units, be sent to Korea. Shipped in two batches, 36 jets went to the 4th FIG at Kimpo. Their mid-November arrival coincided with the movement of the group's third squadron from Japan to its Korean base. The remaining 39 went to Suwon, where the 51st FIG was ordered to transition from its war-weary Shooting Stars. This gave the Fifth Air Force 165 Sabres, with 127 of them based in Korea.

CHAPTER SIX

Most of those that flew the Sabre initially, were veterans of World War II. I, however, was a graduate of the new post war training program for a new breed of jet age fighter pilots. There were two phases to my training. The first was flying a T-6 Texan and then advanced training in a Lockheed T-33. The North American Aviation T-6 Texan was a single-engine advanced trainer aircraft that first flew in 1935 and saw service as a trainer around the world. The initial phase consisted of two weeks of classroom training on the fundamentals of flight and meteorology, before moving on to basic flying training, which initially consisted of mainly touch and go flights around the airport. Once the first solo flight had been completed, we moved onto instrument flying, aerobatics, night flying and cross country flying. We flew yellow T-6G trainers. With 84 hours dual flying and 46 hours solo, I was ready to move onto the next phase at Williams AFB, Arizona for my advanced training on jets. At Williams AFB, there was another two weeks of theory covering high altitude flight and more advanced meteorology. The flying started on a T-6D for two months involving formation flying, more acrobatics, cross country and night flying. Once competent in the T-6, we moved to the T-33 and F-80 shooting star. The T-33 was a trainer developed from the Lockheed F-80 shooting star. The T-33 had a single Allison J33-A-35 centrifugal compressor turbojet. It was a nice aircraft to fly, quite responsive, although also ponderous, especially when compared to the F-86.

I logged 70 hours in the T-6, 26 hours in the T-33 and 39 hours in the F-80. At 265 hours, was finally awarded my pilot's wings. I could now fly, but was still not a fighter pilot. For that I went to Nellis AFB for my F-86 fighter training. Nellis AFB is based in Southern Nevada with the most military schools and squadrons of any other USAF base. Covering 11,300 acres, including weapons ranges and unused area. It has two runways and ramps, big enough for 300 aircraft. Along with recreation, shopping and accommodation for most of its 12,000 military and civilian staff. Again, cross country, formation, and aerobatics were part of the training. This was along with fighter-bomber and air to air combat training. My F-86 conversion training meant I had around 85 hours logged on the F-86, before being sent to Korea.

As for our MiG-15 colleagues, the majority of pilots making up the Soviets' 303rd and 324th IADs had extensive experience in World War II. With more than 300 hours in jet fighters. Although the Americans introduced fresh pilots into their Korean-based F-86 units before the combat veterans rotated home, this meant that new pilots gained valuable experience from Veterans before the Veterans went home. This gave wings with a mixture of veterans and new pilots who were constantly rotated. The Soviets on the other hand replaced whole divisions with Veterans leaving and a new swath of inexperienced pilots joining the war. By 1952, the two highly experienced units were replaced by divisions who had just completed conversion to the high performance, swept-wing MiG-15, and therefore had little experience in the jet, and none in combat. Another issue for the Communists, was as the 303rd and 324th IADs departed, the Chinese-led Ob'yedinyennaya Vozhdushnaya Armiya (OVA or "Unified Air Army") was formed. This was made up of two PLAAF and one KPAF MiG-15 divisions, with the two new, inexperienced, IADs from the USSR's Provito Vozdushnaya Oborona Strany (Air Defence Troops of the Nation or PVO-Strany) attached to it "for their protection". These inexperienced pilots meant for a period of time Sabre pilots had an easier job and their victory tallies increased by quite some margin.

Like American pilot training of the time, Soviet pilot training took around a year. But Stalin sought to minimize the USSR's exposure and risk in its involvement in Korea and wanted the PLAAF to assume responsibility for air operations within the year, so he ordered the V-VS to shorten its initial pilot training program to six months, followed by a "six-month aircraft conversion program to train them to employ Soviet made aircraft and combat techniques."

Soviet, training was more balanced in terms of the amount of theory and practical flying. The American training model had a more practical aspect with much greater hours spent flying than in theory lessons.

Chinese training was far more difficult to achieve due to the 4th to 9th grade education levels of the pilot recruits. The language barrier proved almost insurmountable obstacles in teaching the "peasant soldiers" the complex concepts upon which modern military aviation is based. Even with translators and former KMT aviators assisting each classroom session, it took almost twice as long to teach any subject. This meant that there was no choice but to lower the training standards and theory especially, was reduced.

Each Soviet MiG-15 regiment included two Yak-17UTI straight wing fighter trainers within its ranks. The Yak-17UTI was the only two-seat jet trainer in the V-VS inventory at the time. Four hours of dual instruction was provided, using the YAK-17 before the PLAAF or KPAF student was allowed to fly the single-seat MiG-15.

The V-VS's post-World War II flying training program had two phases – elementary training in the Yak-18 light trainer and basic training in the more robust Yak-11, the 700hp equivalent of the 550hp T-6 Texan. Typically, a Soviet student graduated with 150-180 hours flying time in total, but in the shortened program administered to the PLAAF, Chinese students averaged 27 hours on the Yak-18 and 30 on the Yak-11.

When the first class graduated in October 1950, 120 new pilots were assigned to the first three PLAAF MiG-15-equipped fighter air divisions (the 2nd, 3rd and 4th FADs, with a similar number forming MiG-9 FADs).

Their instruction began with theory lessons on "the design, defects and natural effects" of jet aircraft (16 hours), the design and operation of jet engines (20 hours), radio equipment (six hours) and oxygen equipment (12 hours), and the practical study of the aircraft's cockpit and controls (24 hours). Each training day included seven hours of instruction, which then linked to actual flight training. The flying training began with three additional hours in the Yak-11. Called "clean up", this was to ascertain the student's proficiency, and led directly to four hours of dual instruction in the two-seat, straight-wing Yak-17UTI jet trainer. The Yak-17 was an early single engine jet fighter. It was developed from the Yak-15, the main difference being tricycle landing gear. The trainer version, known as the Yak-17UTI was the most numerous early jet trainer. The YAK-17 was not without its faults with including relatively low speed and range, and an unreliable engine.

With basic flight training completed, the student soloed on the MiG-15, amassing some 16 hours in the type before graduating. By the time a PLAAF MiG-15 pilot completed training, he had a mere 80 hours of flight time, of which only 20 were in jet aircraft. This led to an increase in accidents, through a lack of experience. The PLAAF pilots had none of the formation flying or combat light tactics, taught to American pilot's, further leaving them at a disadvantage in combat.

CHAPTER SEVEN

Korea, called Hanguk in South Korea and Joseon in North Korea, is divided into two distinct sovereign states, North Korea (aka, DPRK or Democratic People's Republic of Korea) and South Korea (aka, ROK or Republic of Korea). Located on the Korean Peninsula, Korea is bordered by China to the northwest and Russia to the northeast. It is separated from Japan to the east by the Korea Strait and the Sea of Japan (East Sea). The adoption of the Chinese writing system in the 2nd century BC and the introduction of Buddhism in the 4th century AD had profound effects on the Three Kingdoms of Korea, which was first united during Silla (57 BC – AD 935) under King Munmu. The united Silla fell to Goryeo in 935 at the end of the Later Three Kingdoms period. Goryeo was a highly cultured state and created the Jikji in the 14th century. The invasions by the Mongolians in the 13th century, however, greatly weakened the nation, which was forced to become a tributary state. After the Mongol Empire's collapse, severe political strife followed. The Ming-allied Joseon emerged supreme in 1388. The first 200 years of Joseon were marked by relative peace and saw the creation of the Korean Hangul alphabet by King Sejong the Great in the 14th century and the increasing influence of Confucianism. During the latter part of the dynasty, however, Korea's isolationist policy earned it the Western nickname of the "Hermit kingdom". By the late 19th century, the country became the object of the colonial designs by Japan. In 1910, Korea was annexed by Japan and remained a colony until the end of World War II in August 1945.

In 1945, the Soviet Union and the United States agreed on the surrender of Japanese forces in Korea in the aftermath of World War II, leaving Korea partitioned along the 38th parallel, with the north under Soviet occupation and the south under U.S. occupation. These circumstances soon became the basis for the division of Korea by the two superpowers, exacerbated by their inability to agree on the terms of Korean independence. The two Cold War rivals then established governments centred on their own respective ideologies, leading to Korea's division into two political entities of North Korea and South

Korea. This division laid the foundations of the War in Korea with North Korea invading South Korea in June 1950. The war and the years that have passed since it, have done nothing to curtail the ongoing North and South tensions.

CHAPTER EIGHT

When the F-86 Sabre appeared, it was the world's fastest jet at 685mph closely followed by the MiG 15 at 670 mph. The performance of the Sabre had the Soviets intrigued and they wanted to capture one in order examine and learn its secrets, which would help the development of their own jet aircraft. The Soviets, wanted to learn everything they could about the aircraft prior to getting their hands on one. Soviet intelligence agents monitored F-86 radio transmissions, interrogated unfortunate Sabre pilots who had been shot down and were now POWs. They then reported their findings to the Soviet leadership, Joseph Stalin, who gave the order to capture a Sabre.

In April 1951, the Soviet Central Aero-Hydrodynamics Institute, a flight research centre located at what is now Zhukovsky Airfield near Moscow, dispatched a special group of test pilots to a training base in Manchuria. The plan was to try and box in a Sabre, before escorting it to Manchuria before trying to force it to land. It would call for precision flying by the MiG pilots and they practiced formation flying.

With a month's worth of practice under their belt, the Soviet pilots joined the 196th Fighter Air Regiment, part of the 324th Fighter Air Division, at Andun, on the Manchurian side of the Yalu River, which formed a border between China and North Korea. However, this proved fruitless in terms of seizing a Sabre. During their first combat experience, on May 31, 1951, one of the senior test pilots was shot down. Then their commander died in a crash landing at Andun airfield within weeks of the first loss. Several members of the group were recalled back to Moscow. Five test pilots remained in theatre and were absorbed into combat units, but the plan to trap and force a Sabre to land was quietly dropped.

Luck finally played into the hands of the Soviets on October 6, 1951, when a Sabre piloted by Bill Garrett performed a belly landing in a tidal pool on the coast of the Yellow Sea, after being shot down. A SA-16 amphibian rescued Garret as the Soviets planned to capture the Sabre. For three hours, American fighters tried to destroy the Sabre, whilst Soviet pilots fought them off, losing seven MiGs in the process.

The race was on to locate the Sabre, before the Americans returned. The Soviet's recruited 500 labourers along with a Russian search team to haul the Sabre from the water. The next day the labourers removed the wings under an overcast sky. However, American ships off the coast spotted the group trying to remove the Sabre and fired on them. At the same time an F-84 reconnaissance aircraft flew of the crash site. The race was still on to remove the Sabre by Dawn. They achieved their target, by finally dismantling the Sabre by 4am. Sabre parts were loaded onto trucks and taken away. The convoy hid in tunnels during the day and only drove at night. The lead truck carrying the Sabres forward fuselage was nearly hit by a B-26 trying to locate the convoy. The lead truck, just made it into a tunnel as a B-26 fired on them.

The convoy finally arrived in Andun and was left there a short while. Those that sat in the cockpit, commented how well laid out the cockpit was. Finally, Sabre serial number 49-1319, arrived at the Air Force Research Flight-Test Institute at Zhukovsky, 22 miles southeast of Moscow, in October 1951. Stalin knew the value of the Sabre to his engineers. It would allow them to copy and modify parts, cutting design costs and more importantly time. Stalin's intention was to copy the Sabre in its entirety, just as the Soviets had done with the B-29. The engineers soon realized the Sabre was equal to the MiG-15 and inferior to the more advanced MiG-17, which was soon due to enter production. The project of reverse-engineering the Sabre, was through a design bureau that never came to fruition along with a reverse engineered Sabre. It was lost among the many projects jockeying for attention and funding in the final years of Stalin's regime.

The Air Force Research Flight-Test Institute proceeded with its analysis of the Sabres systems. Engineers removed each item before they measured, photographed, and drew wiring and engineering diagrams of it. One of the systems that most interested the Russian engineers was the gunsight.

The F-86 had a Sperry APG-30 radar gunsight, which was extremely accurate, up to a range of about 3,000 feet and able to measure the range and compute the lead time required even while the target was manoeuvring. The MiG-15, had a manual system that had been designed in 1939. Sabre pilots during the Korean War pilots credited their gunsight with the advantage they had over MiGs. The Soviets also concluded the sight was much better than the Soviet design. Due to Stalin's regime and the pressure of finding Soviet equipment inferior. Matskevic went on to design a comparable sight for the Soviets. He also designed a warning system that detected the signal from the Sabre's gunsight and alerted the pilot that his aircraft was reflecting the signal back to a pursuer. Based on the same technology as today's police-radar detectors, the system was a simple receiver, mounted on the tail. Not too dissimilar in some respects to the advanced missile warning systems fitted to modern day aircraft. The detector had a range of four to five miles.

In May 1952, Matskevic took 10 sets of his new invention to Korea and began installing them in MiG-15s. It took about three hours to complete each installation. Because it occasionally gave false warnings, pilots initially distrusted the device. Many just turned it off, Matskevic said. But he was soon vindicated: A regimental commander flying over the Yalu heard the device give off a faint tone. He checked his six o'clock position and saw nothing. The tone grew louder, so the pilot craned his neck around to look again. Still nothing. He decided the system was acting up, so he shut it off. A minute later, feeling uneasy, he turned it back on. Now the tone was howling. He then looked back one more time to see two Sabres closing to gun range. As the Sabres opened fire, the MiG pilot banked sharply and escaped with only minor wing damage. Matskevic's detector had proved its worth in battle - word of its accomplishment spread like wildfire, saving the lives of many MiG pilots. Matskevic's warning device and its derivatives became a standard equipment on all Soviet fighters.

As more of the Sabres components were evaluated, suitable components were modified and added to Soviet aircraft. For instance the MiG-15bis, already in production at the time, was given a larger speedbrake and new hydraulic systems to operate the elevator and ailerons. The larger brake and aileron boost system were also incorporated into the MiG-17. The small Sabre accelerometer, for measuring G forces, was adopted and installed on the MiG-19.

As work on the Sabre an F-86A, continued in earnest, an F-86E was shot down over Korea by flak in July 1952. Although the F-86E was in a worse condition it had a newer hydraulic control system that eliminated the cables used in the F-86A. It also used an all-moving horizontal stabilizer. The evaluations of the F-86E, continued after the Korean War had ended.

A prototype of the MiG-17, dubbed SI-10, was selected to evaluate the features of the new F-86E models. After the design bureau test pilots made several flights at Zhukovsky airfield, Mikoyan ferried it to the Chkalovskaya airfield and in June 1955 began testing it. The fully movable stabilizer was also tried on the MiG-17 but only adopted on the MiG-19.

One of the most significant adaptations the Soviets made after capturing the Sabres and Sabre pilots was the introduction of G-suit systems. This enabled Russian pilots to handle the higher G encountered in the MiG and Sukhoi fighter jets which came later. A pilot who could handle higher G could perform more extreme manoeuvres in dogfights, especially true of later jet fighter designs. These more extreme manoeuvres could change the outcome of a close in dogfight at high speed.

CHAPTER NINE

We were on an escort mission today, with a flight of twin propeller B-26 Invaders to escort to their target, B-26s, aircraft that were World War Two veterans. They were sitting ducks against the MiG-15 - without a fighter escort they had very little chance of making it to their target, in between the flak and enemy fighters. Our bombers were still playing catch up to our fighters. The Boing B-47 jet bomber with performance more akin to a jet fighter will take over shortly and the Boeing XB-52 is currently being developed. So I cannot see it being long before the B-29s and B-26s can be retired.

We climbed up to about thirty five thousand over a flight of B-26 Invaders headed up the Yalu River to target a bridge. We constantly scanned the sky for bandits, but, strangely none showed. The B26 s dropped their bombs, with most landing short, but I did see a couple hit the bridge and saw the centre section collapse. A bridge is a small target to hit from high up. We continued to circle as the final B26s made their run and escorted them through a barrage of flak and onto the coast, before letting the bombers complete their journey safely back to base. The B-26s due to being changed from A-26 in 1945, are still confused with the original WWII B-26 Maruader or "Widow Maker" as it was known.

B-26 Invaders of the 3d Bombardment Group, operating from bases in Southern Japan, were some of the first USAF aircraft engaged in the Korean War, carrying out missions over South Korea on June 27 and 28, 1950 before carrying out the first USAF bombing mission on North Korea on June 29, 1950 when they bombed an airfield outside of Pyongyang.

We all had more than enough fuel left to get us back. Whilst over enemy positions we would see if there were any potential ground targets to use up our ammunition on. Very few targets of opportunity came up, but a train snaking its way along, was far too tempting and we dropped down to shoot it up. Going low level had its own dangers, not only from the ground itself and misjudging obstacles or changes in the height of the ground. Bit from enemy small arms fire. A couple well placed rounds could wreak havoc, cutting a control cable or fuel line, worse of all injuring or even killing the pilot.

We swooped down and our target was the large, dirty black steam engine. As had been found in World War Two – hit the boiler and there was a good chance the locomotive would explode in a spectacular fashion, damaging railway infrastructure at the same time. I was second in line to attack the train, I slowed my Sabre down as I descended, using the speed brakes and got the train into the centre of my reticule, before hitting the fire button and spuing out hundreds of rounds, which went on to impact the side of the locomotive. Sadly, no explosion, as I pulled up and tried to quickly regain height, before the third Sabre did a strafing run. The train had slowed down considerably and there was smoke now pouring out of the damaged boiler on the locomotive.

The third Sabre managed to finally get the locomotive to explode I a spectacular fashion as the boiler blew up, due to the high pressure steam it contained. The explosion blew the locomotive and the first three cars clean of the tracks and onto their side. Blocking the line for a few hours and slowly down the movement of supplies. Now, low on ammunition we climbed higher still for the final leg of the journey back to base. We had not got lucky with any MiGs, but at least we had stopped a train in its tracks. Notwithstanding the fact that the B-26s had not only been able to hit their target safely, but get back home without any losses.

After a quick debrief, a coffee and a couple of cheeseburgers it was time for us to get in our rides and fly on another escort mission for a group of F84 Thunderjets. The first strike group was greeted by intense AAA (anti-aircraft artillery) fire. As the second group of Thunderjets made their way out of the area, a group of 16 MiGs appeared on the horizon. One of our flight had to head back after developing a technical fault. Leaving us in a flight of three. For once we had the advantage of height on the MiGs, as normally it was the other way round. We dived right into the middle of the enemy formation. The flight of MiGs started turning and twisting violently to get out of our way. A constant exchange of short burst of fire started. They were shooting us and we were shooting them, when all of a sudden the MiGs decided to pull up and gain altitude. Out of the corner of my eye, I noticed a Thunderjet that had become cut off from his flight, and a MiG-15 was closing in on him for the kill – there was no way a Thunderjet could outrun a MiG. Both of these aircraft were about 4,000ft below us. I immediately rolled over and dived down at full throttle toward the pursuing MiG, hoping to distract him before he got into a good firing position behind the Thunderjet. I fired a burst of fire well out of range of the MiG, as I closed on him. It seemed as though the MiG pilot had seem my tracers; because he quickly turned his aircraft to the right, pulling up into a climb on full throttle. In the meantime, the Thunderjet made a fast and safe exit from the area, whilst I closed on the MiG. I knew I needed to get on his six quickly and hope for a lucky hit to slow him down before my airspeed bled off, with the MiG having a better rate of climb. I knew that as soon as my speed started to drop, the MiG would zoom up and out of range. Suddenly, the MiG pilot reduced his turn. I quickly got my sight lined up with his fuselage and fired. My rounds missed, as I saw them go right under his belly. He tightened his turn again and I put the sight on him again and fired – another near miss. Effectively, the MiG pilot was doing an aerial sideways skid.

For my next aimed shot, I compensated a little for his skidding and pulled the trigger. The six 0.50-cal. guns roared as I held the trigger down and my Sabre gave a slight shudder as the rounds blasted out towards the MiG. What I saw as the rounds impacted was like sparks coming off the ends of a wire. Sparks were coming off the MiGs wing, fuselage and tail. I was so drawn in by what I was seeing, I expended all of my ammunition without realising it. The MiG continued to fly though, as if my rounds had had no effect at all. I called my flight to get whoever was closest to finish the MiG off. I pulled out and checked, there were no other MiGs in sight before Warrior began to get into firing position. The MiG was now constantly changing direction and jinking to avoid being pursued further.

Warrior quickly got a good line of sight and fired off several bursts of fire, one burst hitting the centre fuselage squarely, this caused the MiG to break off and dive to escape, north of the Yalu River. Judging by the way this Mig had been flown, it had to be a Russian pilot. The MiG was full of holes and bits hanging off, was adding drag to the MiG and reducing its speed considerably. Knowing the airframe was nearing its limit, I gambled, that if I got him to undertake a couple more extreme manoeuvres the MiG may well break up.

I pushed the throttle fully forward to some speed so that I could gain on the MiG. It did not take long for me to be gaining on him at quite some pace. The MiG pilot was watching my closure rate, and to avoid me firing on him, unaware I had no more ammunition. The MiG decided to go into a steep dive. Instantly, the MiG started to roll to the right before going down vertically. Part of the structure had given way somehow and the MiG was in a terminal dive. I saw the pilot bail out and his chute pop open, before I gained height and headed back to join my flight and head for home.

CHAPTER TEN

We were waiting at the end of the runway in pairs, 60 seconds apart to avoid jet wash. A T-6 recce plane had been sent out ahead of our attacks to find targets. We had recently been equipped with the F model, which meant not only could we reach the same heights as the MiGs but carry rockets, for harder hitting ground attack. We took off into a clear blue sky, with the slightest of breezes. As soon as we were off the ground we formed up into a flight of four and made our way to our first target. The F model had brought the balance back after the MiG-15bis which had the edge on us previously. The E model had been the first real leap with an improved flight control system and an 'all-flying tail.' The Es improved flight system, basically changed from cables to a full power-operated control with an 'artificial feel' built into the aircraft's controls. To give the same feel as a conventional stick system, but at the same time much lighter at higher G and speed. The F gave us more power with an improved engine and larger wing, again to improve handling and manoeuvrability.

The Sabre had always given us confidence in battle and we had learnt to make use of its strengths. This new model gave us even greater confidence in the Sabre, especially with so many MiGs cruising around. Our older A and B models had been flown to breaking point, it's amazing the wings had not fallen off. A testament to our ground crew for keeping them flying sortie after sortie even when they came back slightly bruised and battered

Our flight climbed out and made cruising altitude. At cruising altitude we got our targets, some large advancing troop positions in need of strafing. Another 10 minutes of flying and we were near our target. One by one we rolled to the left and dived down onto the enemy position. It did not take long to work out what was going on. A North Korean attack was in progress in what looked like a pincer movement to squeeze US troops from either side, in order to crush the remaining ground forces between two tank columns and thousands of soldiers. The wintery conditions with melted snow turning the ground to mush, making it difficult going for tanks, slowing down the advance. The roads had also turned into a mud bath making for difficult going.

Our objective was the tanks and with many forced onto the roads, taking a few out at the front of the column would make the difficult conditions, even more difficult. Any destroyed tanks would have to be moved off the road to continue the advance, further leaving them open to attack from above and well trained artillery fire. We began our strafing run and were soon joined by F-51s better known as the P-51. With the enemy attack stalling, US troops could start to advance once again. As we made several more runs obliterating a dozen or so tanks in the process. Further assets arrived in the form of P-80s and our attention needed to turn to the sky and MiGs coming in to knock out our aerial close support.

As expected as we climbed up four MiGs came screaming down setting my warning buzzer off, to alert I had been locked onto. I had seconds to react before a hail of bullets would rain down on me. I jinked left and threw my Sabre into a tight turn, losing some altitude at the same time. The MiG was still closing in and I had to change direction to try and shake him from my six. With the MiG still closing, I went into a loop, losing valuable speed in the process. As I climbed tracer fire sped past my cockpit and hopefully missed. I went back into a dive before looping up again.

The MiG was right behind me, but in a wider loop. I went straight up, slowing almost to a stall. Instead, I would make use of my speed rakes and see if I could get the MiG to overshoot, it was a dangerous manoeuvre timed wrong, the MiG would have a perfect shot. I slowed right down to almost a stall and it worked the MiGshot passed and I had a few seconds to get rounds off before I stalled and would have to bring the nose down to gather speed. I got the timing perfect, more luck than judgement and got off a few rounds. Enough rounds to cause black smoke to start billowing out of the tailpipe of the MiG. I had no time to watch what happened to the MiG next, as I was about to stall and pushed the nose down to regain some speed and get away.

I spent the rest of my air time finishing of my rockets and ammo on the North Korean forces in full retreat, taking out the retreating troops, tanks, and trucks, making the roads all but impassable. From what I could see, it looked like the advancing Allied troops had broken out of the North Korean trap at the bottom of the peninsula and were moving north at a ferocious pace. Everywhere I looked, something was burning, a truck, a tank, a building. It looked like a complete firestorm on the ground.

Dogfighting in the Korean War, was not that far removed from dogfighting in World War II. Although closer speeds and overall dogfighting speeds were much faster. Here is an account of a P-51 v Me262 encounter during the air war over Europe in WWII:

I went down in a screaming dive, pushing everything forward - throttle, emergency throttle, propeller control and all. The Me262 had a good start, but I had the advantage of several thousand feet more altitude, and was gaining speed by diving. The wind shrieked against my windshield and the Packard Merlin engine bellowed, while the airspeed indicator needle moved steadily around its dial and on up past the four hundred miles an hour mark. The P-51 Mustang controls became heavier as we shot down like a dart. As I drew close to the first Me262, I pulled back on the control column to bring my guns to bear on the wing section, knowing that if I hit an engine I could partially disable or even destroy the Me262 with one pass. Even with a slight pull on the stick I could feel the g effects and my vision blur ever so slightly. I ended up being was a little way behind the 262 when I got down to his level, but I was gaining on him fast, because of the extra speed I had from my dive. I was holding my thumb over the firing button now and keeping my eyes glued to the unmistakable 262 silhouette ahead, except for an occasional glance at the rear vision mirror to see that I wasn't being chased too. I could feel my heart pounding away in my chest as I got within firing range. The 262 grew steadily larger in the circle of my gun sight as I drew closer. I could tell its distance by the amount of space it covered in the sight. After strafing a B-17 and badly damaging it, the Me 262 must have spotted me and began to turn. However, the Mustang could out turn a 262, I just had to ensure that I did not bleed off too much speed and could bring my guns to bear down in the next few seconds. My sights centred on it turning, as I banked slightly to my right and brought the guns to the correct firing position for a deflection hit. I squeezed the firing button with my thumb. B-r-r-rup-pup-u-pup! The sound came to me muffled by my heavy helmet; but it was a venomous sound, and I could feel the Mustang shudder and slow down slightly from the recoil as the six 0.50 calibre M2 Browning machine guns growled and spat out at least one hundred rounds in the one second burst of fire.

I felt the Mustang judder slightly as I hit the wake of the 262, most of which was caused by its jet engines on full power, I could hear them screaming away, as I pulled the stick, and brought the Mustang back on target for a final pass before the 262 could escape due to its greater speed. As it was already starting to pull away. I lined up and hit the fire button for another 1 second burst and scored a fatal hit, smoke began to belch out from the 262s port engine along with a quite obvious wing fire. I did not stick around, not wanting to be hit by debris, should the 262 explode and broke right to put some distance between myself and the 262.

With some distance I could now see the 262 had gone into a shallow dive and was in a slight spiral with flames emanating from the port wing. I have no idea to this day if the pilot managed to escape or not. I just saw the explosion, as the 262 hit the ground and I had chalked up my fourth confirmed kill.

Due to its speed the Me262 was a worthy adversary and if you got bounced, could do some serious damage with its four 30 mm MK 108 cannons.

I must have hit a rookie, as on other occasions I have not been able to catch a 262, but get them in a slow turn and the Mustang had the advantage. The Rookie 262 pilot had slowed down too much to hit a B-17 then had to wait for his engines to spool up and pick up speed. A real 'schoolboy' error that I had been able to take advantage of. My only other 262 kill had been on the ground just as it took off and was picking up speed. This, coupled with the low thrust at slow speeds and high chance of a flameout if the throttle was worked too aggressively, resulted in Me 262 pilots being very vulnerable at takeoff and also being told to avoid low speed dogfights with the Allied piston-engine fighters.

The high speed of the 262 also presented its own problems for pilots when engaging allied aircraft, the high-speed convergence, allowing 262 pilots little time to line up their targets or acquire the appropriate amount of deflection. This same problem faced any aircraft that approaches another from behind at much higher speed, as the slower aircraft in front can always pull a tighter turn, forcing the faster aircraft to overshoot. The 262 faced this problem frequently as its cruising speed alone was up to 120 mph faster than that of any piston-engine fighter of the period. *Luftwaffe pilots eventually learned how to handle the 262's higher speed, and the 262 soon proved a formidable air superiority fighter, with pilots such as Franz Schall managing to shoot down 12 enemy fighters in the Me 262, 10 of them American P-51 Mustangs. We were lucky that the number that entered service was not enough to turn the tide on the war and the lack of experienced pilots and reliability hindered the 262 further.*

262 Pilots soon learned though that the 262 was quite manoeuvrable at higher speeds, despite its high wing loading and lack of low-speed thrust, especially if attention was drawn to its effective manoeuvring speeds. The controls were light and effective right up to the maximum permissible speed and perfectly harmonized. The inclusion of full span automatic leading-edge slats, used on other Messerschmitt fighters dating back to the original Bf 109's on outer wing slots of a similar type. These slats helped increase the overall lift produced by the wing by as much as 35% in tight turns or at low speeds, greatly improving the aircraft's turn performance as well as its landing and take off characteristics. 262 pilots also found that due to the 262s clean design like all jets, it held its speed in tight turns much better than conventional propeller-driven fighters, which was a great potential advantage in a dogfight as it meant better energy retention in manoeuvres.

Extract taken from the authors Dogfight: Battle for the Skies in WWII.

CHAPTER ELEVEN

Our flight consisted of six Sabres as we climbed out and formed up in a finger four formation plus two high on the right. Our job today was another escort mission flying top cover for B29s. At 40,000 feet with the bomber stream below us, we headed toward the target area close to the Yalu River. As we neared the target area eight MiGs appeared on the horizon above our position. With the MiG bases, just minutes away from the combat arena, the MiG-15s usually held the altitude advantage and thus could choose the time and position of their attacks.

"MiGs at one o'clock, angels 50"

We all broke formation and headed towards the MiGs waiting for them to dive down to join us. It was not long before we were in a twisting and turning fierce dogfight. My wingman was trying desperately to get on the tail of a MiG, but the MiG kept on evading him. At the same time, I was playing cat and mouse with another two MiGs, so had no chance of offering any help to my wingman. I got a clean shot at the one I was chasing all and saw him roll out, head down followed in a trail of smoke.

At the same time, I had another MiG on my tail trying to get into firing position, then a hail of bullets hit my wing and port side, with a horrible tearing noise, I had not time to check the damage as the MiG was still on my tail. I went into a steep dive to try to get away, rolling as I did. I had a wounded bird and no was in, full, self-preservation mode, needing to get out of the area and nurse my aircraft home.

I was close to the 38th parallel, hundreds of miles north of the fighting below, at forty thousand feet over enemy territory. The Sabre seemed to be getting heavier and heavier to fly. This could only mean one thing; my hydraulic lines were damaged. My intention, was to stay with my Sabre as long as possible, but that choice was not going to last much longer. I gave the Sabre a little bit of rudder, and the rudder went hard over, pushing me into a spin. Now, I had no choice but to eject, I reached for the red handle and pulled the ejection lever. The explosion blew the canopy off and shot my ejection seat into the air, where I was hit by a 400 mph blast of air. I must have lost consciousness for a moment. Before wakened by a second small blast blew the parachute open. I felt myself being suddenly jerked and flipped over as the parachute grabbed the air and I began my descent into hostile territory. As I floated down, I went through all my options, which were either escape and evade or be captured and become a POW. My attention was now averted to where I was going to land and get myself braced for quite a heavy landing. I just missed a group of trees and landed in a partially snow covered field, that was also knee deep in mud. The mud, however, softened the landing at least, even if it was freezing cold sticky mud. I detached my parachute and began the quite arduous trek across the field and into the trees for better concealment. The chance was quite high, that someone will have spotted my chute coming down, knowing a downed pilot was in the area. Once in better cover I could check my survival kit and see if I could get a message out, to be rescued. Although, my position deep in enemy territory would be a no go or a rescue and I would need to get myself into friendly territory before being captured if at all possible. My best bet, would be try and head for the coast and then follow it round, or possibly steal boat and get away. In my survival kit was a compass, which would be my guide to the coast. As it would be dusk in an hour or so, I decided that I had better get moving and find a safe location to stay for the night, moving during the night would be best. But the chance of getting lost, would grow as well.

    I turned and looked east. Somewhere out there had to be Wonson, a big port city of the North Koreans. I'd make for the beaches just south of Wonson, which I had flown over on many an occasion. Once there, I would easily be able to find a boat of sorts, and make good my escape. After an hour, I found at the bottom of a rocky outcrop, a cave I could spend the night in. It would be cold though, but trying to make a fire was too bigger risk. At least, I was warm now, from my hour trek.

    The early morning sunshine had just broken through, as I popped my head out of the cave, I had just spent the night in. I felt cold and hungry, this survival business when doing it for real, was far harder than in training.

As I made my way in the clear and crisp early morning sunshine, I saw in the distance a small shack with a wisp of smoke curling up from a pipe in the roof. I'd have to make my way around and not chance crossing the field and being seen or heard. Keeping a hundred feet back from the clearing, I crept silently around until I figured I was well beyond the shack. It was late morning now and I had another small building to creep around. As I started to move round the building, a dog barked and I froze. The door to the shack opened. A woman's head poked out and shouted at the dog. She closed the door and went back inside. My heart was nearly, beating in my mouth as I froze and got down as low as possible, doing my best not to be spotted.

With the danger passed, I got up in my mud soaked flying suit and continued onward. The woods were thinning out and there were more cultivated fields than wooded areas the further east I went. I had come across a road, and the temptation as to follow it, as it was far easier to navigate along a road, rather than through fields. The downside was that it greatly increased my chances of being spotted. I decided to chance it and jumped over the ditch between the edge of the field and the gravel road.

I was able to pick up the pace a little using the road, and tucked into a couple of snacks from my survival kit, it did little to cure the hunger, but gave me a little more energy. I had to quickly run for cover when I heard a vehicle coming. The last one had been two soldiers in a small military 4x4, rifles across their laps, eyes peeled on the woods. I was unsure if they were looking for me, or simply just passing through. Either way, I did not want to be spotted, otherwise it would be game over.

CHAPTER TWELVE

It had been 24 hours, since I had been in the relative warmth of my Sabre's cockpit. I was now trudging along a road in North Korea, trying to get back into friendly territory. I had been lucky with the lack of traffic on the road, the odd car and a couple of horses. It was only the Korean voices that had alerted me to the horses, as I made a quick dash for cover in a ditch. I was sure they had seen me, but evidently not. Every few hours I could hear the familiar sound of Sabres flying high, sometimes with B29s and sometimes on their own. A gaggle of F-51s flying low overhead gave me quite a start. I hoped they would see me, but judging by my current appearance, I looked more like a dishevelled farmer than a fighter pilot.

An an hour later, I stumbled and fell twisting my foot in the process. The pain in my foot throbbed. I dragged myself into some woods and sat down, leaning against a fallen log. I fell asleep from sheer exhaustion, when I awoke it was dark. My foot was still swollen, but felt like I could stand on it. I used the trunk of the tree to help support me as I got up and put weight on my foot. I winced a little as the foot took my full weight. I was in need of food and water more than ever, now was the time to think about foraging. My plan was to sneak into an occupied building in the middle of the night and steal something to eat. It went against my ethics, but this was war and I needed to survive.

I got back on the road and within a couple of hours I stumbled upon a small village. All I needed to do was find a house that was unlocked and try to find anything I could to eat. The village was so peaceful and quiet, it was hard to believe a war was going on in the surrounding area.

I skirted around the village and found a house on the outskirts, I could potentially break into and get something to eat. I walked slowly and as silent as possible to the back door and tried it. My luck was in – the door opened with a slight low-pitched creak. I peered into the gloom and the room that lead off the back door was what looked like the kitchen. I was so hungry I could have eaten anything in sight. I saw some fruit and bite into the most delicious apple I have ever tasted. It may well have been a horrible apple, but to me it was the best I had ever tasted. I took a couple of bites before spotting a loaf of bread. Which I just grabbed, along with a bottle of what I hoped was beer or wine. Not wanting to be caught, I made my way quickly out of the house and across a couple of fields to a small group of trees. I had eaten the apple as I was walking and now started munching on the loaf of bread. It tasted different to any bread I had ever had. I took the cap off the bottle and began to drink it, it was what I think is rice wine, though to this day, I am not quite sure. With some food in my stomach and liquid refreshment, I sat under yet another tree on a cold night and grabbed a few hours of sleep.

When I awoke, I was slightly shocked to see a farmer with is Ox ploughing a field, to me it looked like a scene from another century. It obviously had not seen me as he went about his business.

It was my cue to move onward. I wandered through the small forest which came out at a large fast flowing stream. I had no idea how far away a bridge was and the water looked shallow enough to wade through it. As the water got above my ankles, I could feel how cold it was, I continued forward and it was not long before the water was at waist level midstream. I struggle to stand up, such was the force of the fast-moving water. I already felt fatigued and the cold along with the extra effort of wading across the river was getting too much. However, if I tripped or lost consciousness, I would surely drown. I don't know how I made it the final 20 feet to the bank, where I collapsed in a cold and wet heap. I must have passed out as I awoke to the sound of voices. It was two o'clock in the afternoon. All I could do was find somewhere to hide once more. I found a log and crouched down behind it. My leg hurt with cramp, I tried to stretch it out and work my hands over my leg to relieve the pain, slowly the pain died down. I decided to wait behind the log until nightfall before moving on.

As night fell I made my way out of the trees that surrounded a paddy field and waded through the muddy rice paddy and out the other side. I had no idea of how far I had travelled since being shot down, nor how far I had to travel before I would make it to the sea. I knew I was travelling in the right direction by virtue of my compass. I knew I could not go on long this for much longer, my endurance ebbing away each day that passed. I continued through the night, on what was a very dark moonless night and hard to see very far in front of you. I came to what looked like a mound that turned out to be a sand dune. This was the first bit of good news I had had in days. I must be near the sea, but could not see it in the inky black darkness. I decided it would be best to find somewhere to hide until dawn and then work out what to do next.

I sat among some bushes and could hear the sound of the sea gently crashing over the rocks. At dawn I crawled out and made my way to the shore. I could not see any signs of life or buildings. I must have gone slightly wrong and missed the seaside town I was aiming for. My feet were still wet from slogging through the river and they ached quite a bit. I got up and staggered towards the sand dunes and onto the shoreline, hoping to get a sense of direction or better still find a boat I could use. I staggered to the top of the sand dune, my boots struggling to grip the very fine sand.

Once at the top, I lay down on my stomach and scanned the beach in front of me. It was low tide with about a 300 feet of wet sand between the dune and the water's edge. Gentle waves lapped at the shore. To my right, away from the city, the beach meandered along, quite desolate and deserted until it reached a headland where it curved away out of sight. To my left, the beach curved like round towards what I thought was Wonson. I could just make out buildings and would be the best place I could head for. My plan was to get close to Wonson and find somewhere to sleep until nightfall. Wŏnsan is a port city and naval base located in Kangwon Province, North Korea, on the westernmost shore of the Sea of Japan and the provincial capital. The port was opened by occupying Japanese forces in 1880. Before the Korean War, it fell within the jurisdiction of the then South Hamgyong Province.

As I got closer, I could see more houses stretching out in front of me. These towns and villages had looked so different from the air. You never give a second thought about the people living below, and the effects this war is having on their lives. North Korea, to me, seemed to be years behind the USA. But, was that such a bad thing, the people

61

seemed happy enough in their simple day to day lives, or simple I suppose, compared to most of America. About a quarter mile from me, I saw a group of shacks nestled up against the dunes, fisherman's huts, simple and seemingly deserted. On the beach in front of the shacks, where a number of large, rowboats pulled up on the sand above the high tide mark. But, because it was now low tide, they were sitting high and dry a hundred yards away from the water. It would be quite a while before the sea came in and I could steal a boat. It would be hard though, especially if the fishermen came out together, setting up their boats before the tide came fully in.

  The boats were too small for me to climb aboard as a stowaway. I had no choice, but to wait and see. Before, making a decision, as to what I would do next. I decided to move forward, whilst I waited for the tide to move forward and that is what would seal my fate. Blissfully unaware that I had been spotted by some locals out walking, I had not seen them but they had seen me. They had reported it to the Army as having seen a suspicious person behaving strangely. It was not long until the Army had arrived and began their search, whilst I was fast asleep. I was awoken by the jabbing of the muzzle of an AK47 rifle in my ribs, this made me wake up in an instance, sitting bolt upright, before realizing two North Korean soldiers were standing over me shouting something in Korean.

CHAPTER THIRTEEN

I must admit the North Korean soldiers were very friendly and curious about what I was wearing and the equipment I had on me. It was getting dark as the soldiers got me to walk towards a truck that would take me into captivity. My heart sank in one respect, on the other hand, I was so tired, at the time, did not really care that I had been captured. After being taken to another camp I was told to get off and after a quick and most delicious warm drink, I was told to walk with two other soldier's. We must have walked nearly 10 miles through the night.

I was then taken to a prisoner collecting point that a series of tents in the corner of a field. On arrival, the first thing that came into my mind was to escape. I watched and waited to see if there would be any opportunity for me to escape. I had been placed, in what I could best describe as a cage made from wood. I hoped to be able to remove some of the wooden bars, by cutting through the twine holding the cage together. It was very thick twine, even with a stone, proved very hard to cut through.

On the sixth night of my captivity, I very carefully removed a bar and started crawling out. The guard was pacing back and forth just a few feet to my right. I watched him intently watching him, slowly making my way out when I heard soldier's coming up the pathway to the compound. I quickly squirmed back into the cage. I didn't even have time to put the bars in the cage, before the soldiers came to take me out of the cage, blindfolded me, before putting me in a truck with a bunch of South Korean prisoners. We travelled all night on the back of the truck, with three soldiers on guard duty, looking intently at each and every one of us. If I moved too much, a guard would jab me in my shoulder for my trouble.

The next morning we arrived at our next destination and were unloaded and marched into some form of billet for us to sleep. I sat for a while, trying to take it all in, trying to fathom out where I was and what I would do next. Whilst deep in thought, a couple of North Korean Soldiers came in with a very large bowl of rice and placed it down for us all to eat from. All of the prisoners, less me, seemed to have some form of eating utensil, be it with chopsticks or a spoon. I had no choice but to use my hands, until a South Korean prisoner handed me a spoon and I was able to tuck in and eat.

After the rice, which went part way to abating my hunger, I rested for a while, before finding myself being grabbed and blindfolded by two guards and then bundled into a truck all on my own. We travelled all day and into the night before stopping at another North Korean command post. I was pushed off the truck and into the guard house, before being asked all sorts of questions in quite good English, I must say. All I gave was my name, rank and serial number over and over again. I managed to glance out into the cloudy sky and noticed some mountains. This is where I noticed my guards were now Chinese and guarded me round the clock. My new home was an empty room with a hard stone floor, with just a stool and very basic bed. However, I was not allowed to sleep, if I nodded off or lay down, the guards would open the door and start yelling at me in Chinese. This went on for four days, after which they left the door open. They would come in and drag me out two or three times a day for interrogation, I still said nothing. After six days they started to cut down on my food as a further way of torturing me. All I got was a small bowl of rice and a smaller bowl of water each day. On day seven, they would let me go down and bath on a stream and brush my teeth once a day. I still wondered what ultimately would happen to me. I felt broken ad each day was about survival, making it back to my wife and eighteen month old baby. If it were not for them, I may well have given up. I heard nothing from aircraft flying above, nor any sounds of war of any kind. Almost like he war had ended. I had no idea what date it was or even what day it was. Just as I got into the swing of my new routine, I was once again blindfolded and bundled into a truck.

It was nightfall, when I arrived at my new destination, this time I was pushed through some form of hatch into a very small room. When I removed the blindfold, I was in total darkness and had to feel my way around.

I had been put in the cellar of a house and could hear the sounds of boots walking over the top of me. The next morning, I was hauled out of the cellar and taken across a courtyard into another room for a further interrogation. I was with what seemed like more senior Chinese officers, who assured me that due to my lack of co-operation, if I did not answer their questions then I would be shot. I was not sure what to believe and no longer had the energy or the will to care. The one thing I had over them, was my knowledge, with that gone, they had no reason to keep me alive.

After my brief chat, I was taken back across the courtyard and thrown into a dark cell. The room was totally blacked out and I could only see by touch. I guessed I had been brought to a high level interrogation centre, with the thought that what I knew was of great use to someone, somewhere. I knew that now I was in for a much harder time and resigned myself to possibly being killed.

The interrogation process was pretty routine. Once or twice a day they would try to interrogate me. There seemed to be five Chinese and two North Korean interrogators. Once of the North Koreans tried to befriend me by telling me that he was originally from South Korea, but that he had political differences with government officials. Both he and his wife were imprisoned in South Korea. His wife died in prison during childbirth, but he was able to escape, and there was only one place for him to go, and that was to the North. I don't know whether he was sincere or just trying to get me to talk to him.

As well as myself, this interrogation centre had two other American POWs, I had briefly seen both of them, and they looked like they were trying their best not to acknowledge me, possibly for fear of even worse interrogation. I knew the war was still on by the sound of aircraft and battles in the sky above me. I knew this must mean I was near an area of great importance. I was told once that we were next to the Yalu River, even though I had not yet caught a glimpse of the river. Then one day, all the noise in the skies above ceased. A friendly guard told me it was due to an impending ceasfire and I may yet get to go home alive. I had all but given up hope of seeing my home and family, this news buoyed my spirits no end.

About two days later, I was blindfolded along with two others and placed in another truck. We were told us not to talk to each other as we made a short trip to the Yalu River and onto a boat. We sailed through the day and night, stopping to pick up more POWs. Finally, we were ordered off into another camp and the glorious sight of Americans playing basketball. I leapt at the chance to talk and find out what was going on. I was promptly told the war had ended and the North Koreans wanted rid of us as soon as possible. The guards offered me a cigarette, before an officer thrust a questionnaire he wanted filled out. We put down our name, rank, and serial number and handed them back. He became angry and yelling at us. This was the final ploy to get us to reveal information, even though the war had ended, the gathering of intelligence had not.

Apparently, those that had confessed their sins had been given an easy time and those that refused to say anything were given a much harder time. Most of the guys here were pilots with a splattering of enlisted men. It was wonderful to be in the camaraderie of fellow pilots, we all told of how we had come to be shot down and captured and swapped war stories.

One of the guys was an ace, he had shot down his fifth MiG and then ended up being shot down himself. After a couple of days at that camp, we were all put on a train headed south. We went into another compound for a few days, and each day they would take a few guys out to be repatriated. I came out the next to the last day of the repatriation cycle. The thing that impressed me the most as we entered Freedom Village were two husky Military Police who were immaculately dressed from head to toe. The folks running the place questioned us a bit, fed us, and let us make phone calls home.

I was put on a hospital ship to come home. I weighed around 160 pounds when I was shot down and about 100 before repatriation. On the hospital ship, I finally got to rest and recuperate. It was strange to have such comfort, after such a long time in appalling and inhuman conditions. I spoke to those that had given in to the interrogation and those that at held out, it was interesting to hear the rationale for 'spillng the beans' be it threats to their family or simply deciding to give false information, knowing some of it would end up back in Russia.

All of us went through a counter-interrogation on the boat. I was hospitalized after reaching the States and went through another interrogation. When I got to my next base, I went through a third one. Several months after I got home, I received a letter from the Air Force stating that my conduct as a POW was considered commendable and wishing me future success in the Air Force, I decided to stay in the USAF, on my return to America, as my passion was still to fly and fly I did, getting out just before the Vietnam War. My time flying the Sabre is still the time I remember the most. I still rate the Sabre as one of the best aircraft I have ever flown, it was the last great 'dogfighter' in many ways for a number of years, as Air Force politics and policy got in the way of aircraft design.

CHAPTER FOUTEEN

The F-86 and MiG-15 were the first of a new breed of jet fighters, following on from the piston engine dogfights of World War II and early jets. The jet age came along in quite a spectacular fashion. The two-and-a-half-year battle in the air over the Yalu was the struggle for aerial superiority over the rear areas of the Communist military forces in Korea. Air superiority is achieved, by denying the enemy the use of aircraft or even severely limiting their ability to conduct aerial operations. Offensively, of course, it is achieved when air superiority fighters enable friendly air operations to consistently strike their objectives without interference from enemy air forces. The USAF struggle in the bombing campaign by using unsuitable B-29 bombers, that when compared to the jet fighters were slow and ponderous. Their slow speed, made it difficult for the Sabres to easily protect and allow unimpeded aerial operations. The F-86 Sabre could not achieve air superiority against the MiG-15 for the B-29 either, although it did allot to hold the MiGs back and prove itself as a formidable first generation jet fighter. The MiG-15bis led onto the MiG-17 that took the MiG-15bis as a basis and made it better, including an afterburning VK-1F turbojet engine for higher speed without any loss of the MiG-15s manoeuvrability. It even proved itself against the American F-105 and F-4 Phantom during the Vietnam War 12 years later

The F-86, led to the F-100 Super Sabre a supersonic fighter, first flying in 1953 and making wide scale use of Titanium for the first time in a fighter. This aircraft would also see service in Vietnam, in the fighter bomber role.

After October 1951, it was fighter-bombers that carried the UNC's aerial campaign to the enemy, and for the rest of the war there were no F-80C or F-84E fighter-bomber strikes against any target in North Korea disrupted or defeated by MiG-15s.

MiGs never really challenged the Sabres dominance of Mig Alley, this was due to a multitude of factors, from differences of training to deployment and tactics, with the actual aircraft being so evenly matched overall.

The turning point for air superiority for the Sabre was the raid on the Supang Hydro Electric facility in June 1952. This event provided the Sabre with, finally achieving air superiority within this hotly contested arena. From that mission on – with the Soviet MiG forces gradually being withdrawn from the confrontation. The less well trained and less experienced PLAAF started to experience increased and heavy losses. This finally gave, air dominance for the F-86F. From this it is not hard to state that the Mi-15bis was more than a match for the Sabre, however the pilots, in particular the PLAAF were not. The Russian pilots could hold their own against experienced veteran USAF pilots and a comparison of the number of losses and kills by the Soviet and PLAFF pilots.

The lessons learned during the Korean War proved invaluable not only in having combat experienced flying instructors, after the war, but also the knowledge and lessons learned from combat. This knowledge and experience would be passed on to generations of fighter pilots. However, some of these skills were lost with the belief that guns could be replaced with missiles such as the sidewinder. This meant fighters were no longer designed to fight in close dogfights and aircraft like the F-4 Phantom had the power and speed, but lacked the manoeuvrability of its fore bares. Soviet fighters retained their guns and manoeuvrability with the Mig-19 and Mig-21. It would take the F-15 and F-16, to see the return of both guns and the manoeuvrability that would take its pilots to their G limits and bring back 'true' fighter aircraft in fighter pilot's eyes.

The overall conclusion must be that the MiG-15bis and F-86A/ E/ F were nearly equally matched fighters, and the difference, made much more apparent in later months, was provided by the training, experience and morale of the men flying them. From their perspective, aircraft designers on both sides drew conclusions that drove subsequent fighter designs. The Soviets reversed engineered the F86 learning its secrets and using them to improve the MiG-15 and MiG-15bis which was matched by the F-86F The Soviets then sought to beat the F-86F by developing the MiG-15bis45, which became the MiG-17. The next fighter to follow the MiG-17 was the MiG-19.

American designers also wanted to keep up and outperform the early MiGs with the F-100 Super Sabre achieving this, as well as solving the F-86' s the unresolved issue of lacking enough firepower, by mounting four 20mm cannon for its armament.

The F-104, essentially a missile with wings was the brainchild of Kelly Johnson, and gave a high altitude, high performance fighter, but lost the manoeuvrability that gave the MiG-21 the edge and ability to thrash the F-104. The legacy of the F-86 ad the lessons learned both during and after the Korean War has helped shape fighter design. Fighter design is still advancing, with the F-22 Raptor, pushing boundaries along with high production costs and the F-35 Lightning II, demonstrating a lower cost single engine platform adapted to VTOL, Naval and as a conventional fighter. But the MiG-15 also needs to be remembered for the Soviets ability, to find solutions to weaknesses, even if, by using some stolen reverse engineered US technology, but the basis of good fighter design has echoed through the years. With the more recent Su-27 and MiG-29 demonstrating Russia's ability to produce fighters that can still dominate the skies in the right hands.

GLOSSARY

AK47 – The AK47 Kalashnikov assault rifle more commonly known as the AK-47 or just AK (Avtomat Kalashnikova – 47, which translates to the Kalashnikov automatic rifle, model 1947), and its derivatives. It had been and still is with minor modifications, manufactured in dozens of countries, and has been used in hundreds of countries and conflicts since its introduction. The total number of the AK-type rifles made worldwide during the last 60 years is estimated at 90+ million. The AK47 is known for its simplicity of operation, ruggedness and maintenance, and unsurpassed reliability even in the most inhospitable of conditions.

Boeing B-29 Superforteress - The B-29 Superfortress was a four-engine heavy bomber designed by Boeing, it flew towards the end of WWII over Japan and in the Korean war. It first flew on Septemeber 21, 1942 and entered service in 1944. It was powered by four Wright R-3350-23 and 23A Duplex Cyclone turbosupercharged radial engines, developing 2,200hp each. Perhaps the most famous B-29 is the Enola Gay, which dropped the atomic bomb "Little Boy" on Hiroshima on August 6, 1945. With a top speed of 357mph and a range of 2250 miles.

Boeing B-50 Superfortress - The B-50 Superfortress strategic bomber was a post–war revision of the Boeing B-29 Superfortress, fitted with more powerful Pratt & Whitney R-4360 radial engines, stronger structure, a taller fin, and other improvements. It was the last piston-engined bomber designed by Boeing for the United States Air Force.

Boeing B-47 – The Boeing B-47 was a long range, six engine, jet-powered strategic bomber designed to fly at high subsonic speed and at high altitude to avoid enemy interception. The B-47's primary mission was to drop nuclear bombs on the Soviet Union. It first flew on December 17, 1947 and entered service in June 1951, with some initial teething problems. It stayed in service as a bomber until 1965 and was still being used as a reconnaissance aircraft until 1969. Powered by six

General Electric J47-GE-25 turbojets, each rated at 7,200 lbf thrust, giving a top speed of 607mph and a range of 2,013 miles.

Boeing B-52 – The Boeing B-52 is a long range eight engine strategic bomber, which essentially followed on from the B-47. Its first flight was on April 15, 1952 and later versions still remain in service today. Powered by eight Pratt & Whitney TF33-P-3/103 turbofans, each rated at 17,000 lbf of thrust. Top speed is 650mph and a range of 4,480 miles.

Douglas C-54 Skymaster - Douglas C-54 Skymaster was a four-engined transport aircraft used by the United States Army Air Forces in World War II and the Korean War. It was based on the DC-4, and firs flew in 1942 and was retired in 1975. Powered by Pratt & Whitney R-2000-9 radial engines with 1,450 hp. It had a top speed of 275mph and a range of 4000 miles.

General Dynamics F-16 'Fighting Falcon' – The F-16 is a single engine supersonic, multirole fighter aircraft, developed for the USAF. It first flew in January 1974 and is powered by a single F110-GE-100 afterburning turbofan engine. It is one of the most manoeuvrable aircraft in the world and is used by the U.S. Air Force Thunderbirds display team and has been exported to quite a few air forces around the world. With top speed of Mach 1.2 and a range of 2,260 miles with drop tanks.

Lockheed Martin F-22 Raptor - The Lockheed Martin F-22 Raptor is a single-seat, twin-engine, all weather stealth tactical fighter aircraft. The aircraft was designed primarily as an air superiority fighter, but has additional capabilities, including ground attack, electronic warfare, and signals intelligence roles. The F-22 first flew on September 7, 1997. Designed to be stealthy it is powered by two Pratt & Whitney F119-PW-100 pitch thrust vectoring turbofans. With a top speed on afterburner of Mach 2.25, it is also capable of supercruise (Supersonic flight, without afterburner like Concorde) of Mach 1.82. It has a range of 1,840 miles.

Lockheed Martin F-35 Lightning II - is a family of single-seat, single-engine, all weather stealth multirole fighters undergoing testing and final development. The fifth generation combat aircraft is designed to perform ground attack, reconnaissance, and air defence missions. The F-35 has three main models - the F-35A conventional takeoff and landing (CTOL) variant, the F-35B short take-off and vertical-landing (STOVL) variant, and the F-35C carrier-based CATOBAR (CV) variant. It first flew on 15 December 2006. Powered by a single Pratt & Whitney F135 afterburning turbofan with 28,000 lbf dry and 43,000 lbf of thrust with afterburner. It has a top speed of Mach 1.6 and a range of 1,200 nautical miles.

Lockheed P-38 Lightning - The Lockheed P-38 Lightning was a World War II fighter aircraft. Developed to a United States Army Air Corps requirement, the P-38 had distinctive twin booms and a single, central nacelle containing the cockpit and armament. The P-38 was used in a number of roles, including dive bombing, level bombing, ground-attack, night fighting, photo reconnaissance missions, and extensively as a long-range escort fighter when equipped with drop tanks under its wings. It was powered by two Allison V-1710-111/113 V-12 turbo supercharged piston engines, producing 1,600 hp. It had a top speed of 414 mph and a range of 1,300 miles.

Lockheed P-80 Shooting Star – The Lockheed P-80 Shooting Star was the first jet fighter used operationally by the United States Army Air Forces (USAAF). Designed and built by Lockheed in 1943 and delivered just 143 days from the start of the design process, production models were flying, but not ready for service by the end of World War II. It saw extensive service in the Korean war and the designation changed slightly to become the F-80. Powered by a single Allison J33-A-35 centrifugal compressor turbojet, developing 5,400 lbf of thrust. It had a top speed of 600mph and a range of 1200 miles.

McDonnell Douglas F-4 Phantom II - The McDonnell Douglas F-4 Phantom II is a tandem two-seat, twin-engine, all-weather, long-range supersonic jet interceptor fighter/fighter-bomber originally developed for the United States Navy by McDonnell Aircraft. It first entered service in 1960 with the U.S. Navy. Proving highly adaptable, it was also adopted by the U.S. Marine Corps and the U.S. Air Force. The F-4, like other interceptors of its time, was designed without an internal cannon. Later models incorporated an M61 Vulcan rotary cannon. Beginning in 1959, the F-4 set 15 world records for in-flight performance, including an absolute speed record, and an absolute altitude record. Powered by two General Electric J79-GE-17A axial compressor turbojets, each with 11,905 lbf dry thrust and 17,845 lbf in afterburner. The Phantom is a large fighter with a top speed of over Mach 2.2 and a range of 422 miles on internal fuel.

McDonnell Douglas F15 'Strike Eagle' – The F15 Strike Eagle is an all-weather multirole fighter, derived from the McDonnell Douglas (now Boeing) F-15 Eagle. It is powered by two Pratt & Whitney F100-229 afterburning turbofans, 29,000 lbf and capable of Mach 2.5 (2.5 the speed of sound). It first flew in December 1986 and an F15SG version is on order by the ordered by the Republic of Singapore Air Force (RSAF). The F-15 has a top speed of Mach 2.5 and a range of 3,450 miles with external fuel tanks.

Martin B-26 Marauder - B-26 Marauder was a World War II twin piston engine medium bomber built by the Glenn L. Martin Company. It first flew on November 25, 1940. After entering service with the U.S. Army, the aircraft received the reputation of a "Widowmaker" due to the early models' high rate of accidents during takeoff and landings. The Marauder had to be flown at exact airspeeds, particularly on final runway approach and when one engine was out. It was powered by two

Pratt & Whitney R-2800-43 radial engines, rated at 2,000-2,200 hp. With a top speed of 287mph and a range of 1,150 miles.

MiG-17 - The Mikoyan-Gurevich MiG-17 is a high-subsonic fighter aircraft produced in the USSR from 1952 and operated by numerous air forces in many variants. It is an advanced development of the very similar appearing MiG-15. It is still in limited use. Powered by a single Klimov VK-1F afterburning turbojet. Producing 5,046 lbf of thrust dry and 7,423 lbf with afterburner. It has a top speed of 711 mph and a range of 1,280 miles with drop tanks.

MiG-19 - The Mikoyan-Gurevich MiG-19 is a Soviet second-generation, single-seat, twin jet-engined fighter aircraft. It was the first Soviet production aircraft capable of supersonic speeds in level flight. It first flew on Septemeber 18, 1953and still in service with North Korea. Powered by two Tumansky RD-9B afterburning turbojets, with 7,178 lbf of thrust. It has a top speed of 909mph and a range of 860 miles with external tanks.

MiG-21 – The MiG-21 is a single seat, single engine supersonic jet fighter aircraft, Early versions are considered second-generation jet fighters, while later versions are considered to be third-generation jet fighters. Approximately 60 countries over four continents have flown the MiG-21, and it still serves many nations a half-century after its maiden flight. Powered by a single Tumansky R25-300 with 9,040 lbf thrust dry, and 15,650 lbf of thrust with afterburner. It has a top speed of Mach 2 and a range of 751 miles on internal fuel.

MiG-29 - The Mikoyan MiG-29 is a twin engine jet fighter aircraft designed in the Soviet Union as an air superiority fighter during the 1970s. The MiG-29, along with the larger Sukhoi Su-27, was developed to counter new American fighters such as the McDonnell Douglas F-15 Eagle, and the General Dynamics F-16 Fighting Falcon. It first flew on October 6, 1977. While originally oriented towards combat against any enemy aircraft, many MiG-29s have been furnished as multirole fighters capable of performing a number of different operations, and are commonly outfitted to use a range of air-to-surface armaments and precision munitions. Powered by two Klimov RD-33 afterburning turbofans, with 18,300 lbf of thrust each. The MiG-29 has a top speed of Mach 2.25 and a range of 888 miles on internal fuel.

Republic F-84 Thunderjet – The Republic F-84 Thunderjet was an American turbojet fighter-bomber aircraft. Originating as a 1944 United States Army Air Forces (USAAF) proposal for a "day fighter", the F-84 flew in 1946. Although it entered service in 1947, the Thunderjet was plagued by so many structural and engine problems that a 1948 U.S. Air Force review declared it unable to execute any aspect of its intended mission and considered canceling the program. The aircraft was not considered fully operational until the 1949 F-84D model and the design matured only with the definitive F-84G introduced in 1951. Powered by one Allison J35-A-29 turbojet, developing 5,560 lbf of thrust. With a top speed of 622mph and a range of 1000 miles.

Sukhoi SU-27 - The Sukhoi Su-27 is a Russian twin-engine supermaneuverable fighter aircraft designed by Sukhoi. It was intended as a direct competitor for the large United States fourth-generation fighters, with a 1,910 nautical mile range, heavy armament, sophisticated avionics and high manoeuvrability. It first flew on 20 May 1977 and is powered by two Saturn/Lyulka AL-31F turbofans with afterburner, giving a top speed of Mach 2.35.

Yak 7- The Yakovlev Yak-7 was a WWII single engined piston fighter. It was developed from the earlier Yak-1 fighter, initially as a trainer, but converted into a fighter. As both a fighter and later reverting to its original training role, the Yak-7 proved to be a capable aircraft and was well liked by air crews. The Yak-7 was simpler, tougher and generally better than the Yak-1. It first flew on July 23, 1940 and became operational in 1942. Powered by a single M-105PA V-12 liquid-cooled piston engine, developing 1,050 hp, with a top speed of 308 mph, with a range of 400 miles.

Yak 9 - The Yakovlev Yak-9 was a WWII single-engine piston fighter. Fundamentally a lighter development of the Yak-7 with the same armament. It first flew in the Summer of 1942 and was powered by a Klimov VK-107A V-12 liquid-cooled piston engine, developing 1,500 hp, with a top speed of 417mph and a range of 420 miles. During 1949, the Soviet Union provided surplus Yak-9P aircraft to some satellite states in the Soviet bloc in order to help them rebuild their air forces in the wake of the West Berlin blockade. These aircraft were used in the Korean War.

Printed in Great Britain
by Amazon